THE VISITOR'S GUIDE TO
THE PEAK DISTRICT

Visitor's Guide Series

This series of guide books gives, in each volume, the details and facts needed to make the most of a holiday in one of the tourist areas of Britain and Europe. Not only does the text describe the country-side, villages, and towns of each region, but there is also valuable information on where to go and what there is to see. Each book includes, where appropriate, stately homes, gardens and museums to visit, nature trails, archaeological sites, sporting events, steam railways, cycling, walking, sailing, fishing, country parks, useful addresses — everything to make your visit more worthwhile.

Other titles already published or planned include:
The Lake District (revised edition)
The Chilterns
The Cotswolds
North Wales
The Yorkshire Dales
Cornwall & The Isles of Scilly
Devon
East Anglia
Somerset and Dorset
Guernsey, Alderney and Sark
The Scottish Borders
 and Edinburgh
The Welsh Borders
Historic Places of Wales
The North York Moors, York and
 the Yorkshire Coast
South and West Wales
Kent
Hampshire and The Isle of Wight
Sussex
Dordogne (France)
Brittany (France)
Black Forest (W Germany)
The South of France
Tyrol
Loire
French Coast

KEY FOR MAPS

Towns · Villages	
Motorways	
Main Roads	
Peak Park Boundary	
County Boundary	
Rivers	
Canals	
Railways	
Lakes/Reservoirs	
Museum/Art Gallery/Centre	
Cave	
Archaeological Site	
Building/ Country Park Gardens	
Castle/Fort	
Ecclesiastical Building	
Picnic Site	
View point	
Information	
Other Place of Interest	

The Visitor's Guide To
THE PEAK DISTRICT

Lindsey Porter

British Library Cataloguing in
Publication Data

Porter, Lindsey
    The Visitor's Guide to the Peak
    District
    1. Peak District (England) -
    Description and travel — Guide-
    books
    I. Title
    914.25'1104858   DA670.DA

'Good God how sweet are all things here'.
                        Charles Cotton 1676

In memory of my mother W. Hope Porter
(1924-79) and her brother, Arthur Gold-
straw (1906-77) who encouraged my interest
in the countryside, and history of the Peak
District.

ISBN 0 86190 127 4
ISBN 0 86190 126 6 Pbk

Printed in the UK by Butler and
Tanner Ltd, Frome for the publishers
Moorland Publishing Co Ltd, 9-11
Station Street, Ashbourne,
Derbyshire, DE6 1DE England.
Telephone: (0335) 44486

Contents

Acknowledgements 6
Introduction 7
1 The South-West 11
2 The Dove and Manifold Valleys 31
3 South of the Wye 54
4 The Northern Limestone Plateau 73
5 The Derwent Valley 95
6 The Dark Peak 112
Further Information 132
Index 152

Acknowledgements

During the preparation of this book, I received assistance on the walks in the northern moors from Colin Macdonald. Andrew Greenwood of the Information Department of the Peak Park Joint Planning Board and Alex Youell, now with the National Trust, read the draft and offered advice. The information centre staff at Ashbourne and Ruth English at Leek assisted me with my enquiries and my secretary Jan Cundy put up with unfair demands on her working capacity. I am grateful to them all.

The spelling of some of the placenames in this book does not necessarily agree with the spellings adopted by the Ordnance Survey or local highway departments. Consequently alternatives will be found for Three Shires Head, Ludchurch, Alstonfield, Beresford Dale and Youlgreave.

Walks are indicated by a vertical line in the margin, with approximate times and distances. All walks are of a moderate degree of difficulty except those on the northern moors which range from hard to extremely hard depending on conditions.

Black and white illustrations have been provided by: J. Robey; 16, 17, 19, 33, 35, 43, 45, 48 (top), 57, 59, 61, 64, 65, 68, 71, 72, 77, 80, 82, 84, 85, 86, 89, 104, 108, 109, 110: Sheffield Newspapers Ltd; 124, 125, 126: H.M. Parker; 130: Chatsworth House Trust; 106, Back cover: Peak Park Joint Planning Board; 102, 128. The rest are from the author's collection. Colour illustrations have been provided by: J. Robey and the author. Front cover: Peak Park Joint Planning Board;

Introduction

In recent years there has been a marked increase in the number of publications on the Peak District, some of doubtful accuracy. Why then another one? Despite this wealth of literature, there is no one publication which aims to aid the visitor by offering advice as to how to make the most of a visit or holiday in the area. This book tries to fill that gap, but it is not, of course, entirely comprehensive. For one thing, commerical considerations dictate what is available and new attractions occur each season. There is also the question of taste and preference and, of equal importance, the fact that the author is a local historian rather than a naturalist. There is still room for a rambler's guide to the area written by a natural historian, but this may mean identifying the localities of rare species and cause a conflict of interest. Indeed, it has been formally suggested that this book exclude even a list of nature reserves, such is the sensitivity to over-usage. Except where these reserves are well known, this has been respected.

The Peak District lies at the southern end of the Pennines surrounded by the cities of Sheffield to the north-east, Manchester to the north-west, Stoke-on-Trent to the west and Derby to the south-east. Although the Peak is often regarded as being wholly in Derbyshire it must be remembered that large areas to the west are in Staffordshire, indeed Dovedale is the county boundary here and some of the most spectacular scenery is on the Staffordshire bank, while north-west of Buxton, a significant area of the Peak lies in Cheshire.

The rich diversity of scenery has long been an attraction for visitors, sufficient to move the hearts and pens of many nationally-known writers over the centuries. Nowadays, for convenience, the area is often sub-divided into the White Peak and the Dark Peak, each with its own quite distinct character.

The White Peak, defined very approximately as the countryside enclosed by the towns of Buxton, Castleton, Bakewell, Matlock and Ashbourne, is a limestone plateau of green fields and white stone walls. This upland is dissected by the rivers Derwent, Wye, Dove, Manifold and their tributaries to give the region's well-known dales, some with spectacular limestone rocks and cliffs. Dovedale, Manifold Valley, Chee Dale, Monsal Dale, Lathkilldale and the Matlock Gorge are all deservedly popular beauty spots, while there are many more lesser known dales, many now 'dry' without their rippling trout streams, which are a delight to explore.

To the north along the eastern and western margins of this limestone plateau lies the Dark Peak — open heather clad moors of gritstone and shale with a peaty acid soil, a less hospitable area left to the sheep and grouse. This is the country loved by the rambler who wishes to 'get away from it all' and the rock gymnasts who delight in scaling the numerous gritstone 'edges'. But even this area is served by many minor roads, so that the less energetic can park easily and take a gentle stroll along the top of one of the edges with magnificent views over the surrounding countryside.

Couple all this with a rich historical

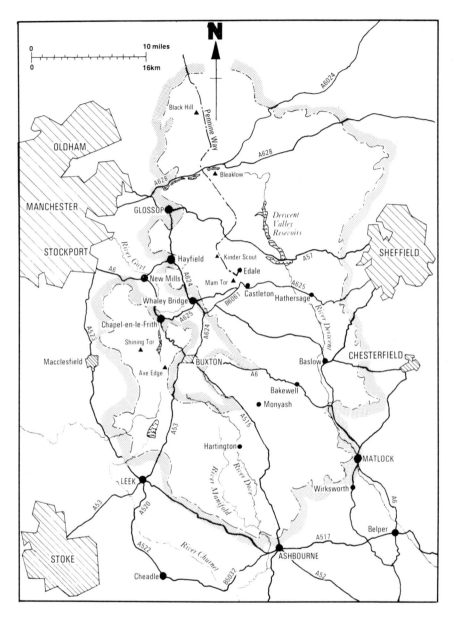

background of stately homes, show caves, ancient lead mines, picturesque watermills, a network of old packhorse way and numerous small towns and villages to explore, then it becomes clear why the Peak District is perhaps the most used (some would say over-used) national park in Britain.

Over-usage of places such as Dovedale, the Pennine Way path over Kinder Scout and Stanage Edge is causing erosion and degeneration of paths to a point at which they are no longer acceptable to many visitors. If this book succeeds in its aim of making visitors aware that there are other areas of equal importance and attractiveness, then its publication will be justified. The thing most country-lovers seek, or seem to seek, is fine rural surroundings accompanied by a certain degree of solitude. One cannot overstress that there are so many area in the Peak where this can be achieved if one looks beyond such beauty spots as Dovedale.

Throughout this book, repeated mention is made of the OS map, or Ordnance Survey Map to give its full title, and Grid Reference numbers. It is essential to carry the maps called 'The White Peak' and 'The Dark Peak'. They contain such a wealth of information for visitors that they are indispensable. Do not be put off by thinking that you can not read a map, for a little practice will show you how easy it really is.

A look at a large map will show vividly the point made above relating to the geographical location of the Peak District National Park. It is unique in that its 542 sq miles are surrounded by one conurbation after another. In fact, some 17½ million people live within 50 miles of the region and the Park attracts 20 million visitors per year. But this book is not confined to a study of the Park itself. There are large areas of interest which are beyond its boundaries, but are included here; the Churnet Valley is a specific example.

The Peak District National Park came into being as a result of the *National Parks and Access to the Countryside Act* of 1949. This was a result of pressure brought to bear on politicians, but its grass roots and geographical base was the Peak District. The National Park which became established differed from others (except the Lake District) in that

it was vested with control over planning matters as well as having responsibility for providing information services to visitors. The Peak Park Joint Planning Board's policies often conflict wth the pressures of society, particularly industry, and restrictions on residential development have contributed to high property prices. This, combined with other important factors, eg decline in agriculture, has resulted in a gradual depopulation of rural communities, particularly among young people. This vicious circle then makes schools redundant, and young people seek a life amongst their own age group in towns. There is no easy solution to this and on balance one has to admit that the establishment of the Board came just at the right time and that its policies have been to our advantage.

The Board also produces a considerable amount of literature on the area, much of it being for schools and some of it in French, Italian, Dutch and German. These leaflets are quite useful and informative to more than schoolchildren and can be obtained directly from the Board at Bakewell or from its information centres, including its mobile caravan which can be found at agricultural shows etc. Amongst the wealth of other publications, five books stand out, being based upon original research and comprehensive in their approach. They are *The Peak District* by Millward and Robinson (Eyre Methuen); *The Peak District* by Christian (David & Charles); *The Peak District* by Edwards in the New Naturalist series, now a Fontana paperback; *Peakland Roads and Trackways* by A.E. & E.M. Dodd and *Wild Flowers and other plants of the Peak District* by Anderson and Shimwell (the latter two titles both by Moorland Publishing). There are of course defintive books on other disciplines such as geology, but these books are recommended for a good general background to the area. There are plenty of walkers'guides to the Peak District, including one by this author. An attempt has been made to include a fair selection of walks in this book, which can easily be extended or shortened to suit particular needs by using the OS map and following other rights of way. The 2½in or 1:50,000 scale maps show every field and with the whole of the Peak almost entirely on two maps it is possible to sort out all manner of routes with comparative ease.

The Peak has been crossed by a countless number of old roads and packhorse ways which have now degenerated to bridlepaths or footpaths. This is an important legacy which we are most fortunate to have. It means that we can leave the car and really get to know an area on paths now little used.

Such is the network of paths that in some areas there is no difficulty on finding circular routes in order to return to the car. Good parking areas are provided in many places and are marked on the White Peak map. At this point perhaps one should stress a word of warning. The maps indicate quite readily just how proliferous are the old lead mines in the area. These present few problems to the rambler so long as they are avoided. If you must know how deep a shaft is, throw lighted paper down it not stones. On no account enter mine workings or caves without an expert, or remove the stone capping a shaft, or for that matter, climb rock faces. The caving and mountain rescue posts were not established without good reason and a memorial at Castleton to Neil Moss is a reminder that all who go underground do not necessarily return. Rock faces and the northern moors have also claimed their share of lives; it is all a case of being sensible.

Finally, please remember that when the visitor has gone home the local has to live and work in the Peak. Respect his property and privacy, his animals and crops and remember the adage: leave only footprints, take only photographs; and have an enjoyable time.

1 The South-West

General Description

The south-western edge of the Peak District is an area of open and often treeless moorland dissected by three river systems — the Churnet, Dane and Goyt. Flowing off the high moors, these three major valleys offer good walking, extensive views and considerable pleasure. There is also much to see. The huge outcrops of rocks known as the Roaches are perhaps the most notable geographical feature. Man has however added much else — the reservoirs of the Goyt and at Tittesworth, interesting market towns, preserved mills and the majestic Tudor Gothic mansion of Alton Towers. One is tempted to single out particular parts of the valleys for special comment, but this would perhaps be misleading for all three are very attractive in their own particular way. There are no contrasting features like those found in the Dove and Manifold, for instance, where sandstones and shales give way to the harder limestone. Here, all the rocks are different varieties of sandstone and shales. It is therefore a different kind of topography moulded in softer rock from the limestone, creating rugged heather and bilberry clad moors in the upper valleys. Further downstream, wooded and often deep, wide valleys are more characteristic.

The Churnet rises to the east of the Roaches and Ramshaw Rocks, flowing into Tittesworth reservoir. Standing on the road bridge at Meerbrook, over the northern end of Tittesworth, the water looks like a huge mirror for the Roaches escarpment behind. To the east rises the ridge known as Morridge, with the

Mermaid Inn standing out on the treeless skyline. Just to the north of the inn is the Mermaid Pool, traditionally said to be bottomless and the home of a mermaid. It is strange that a pool very similar to this and known as Doxey Pool also exists on the Roaches. Near the inn is the headquarters of the Staffordshire Gliding Club and their gliders can often be seen at weekends high over the infant Churnet.

The Axe Edge moors afford good views over quite a large area. From the layby just south of the Mermaid Inn on Morridge one can, for instance, see to the Welsh Hills and the Wrekin in Shropshire on a clear day. The more immediate view down to the Roaches and Ramshaw Rocks is perhaps more spectacular. If your route takes you up the Leek-Buxton road past Ramshaw Rocks, drive slowly looking for the rock which obviously resembles a face. It is known as the Winking Eye rock and it does just that!

Below Tittesworth reservoir, the river skirts the old market town of Leek. The water has for centuries been used for power and for its very pure qualities. The Cistercian monks built the largest abbey church of their order in England on the banks of the river Abbey Green, Leek and also established a watermill, presumably to grind corn. The abbey is no more, but a now preserved cornmill still stands on the site of the original mill, and is referred to later.

At Leek, the river sweeps in a huge arc around the town, meandering out almost to Rudyard where it flows back towards the town in a very deep valley

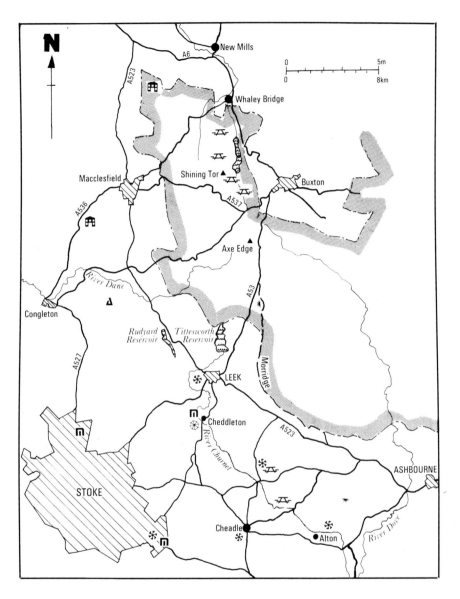

carved out by overflow waters from a glacial lake, known as Lake Dane, that was situated just to the north of Rudyard Lake. A good place to view this is from the Leek to Stoke-on-Trent road (the A53) where it crosses the river. Below Cheddleton, where another preserved watermill exists, the valley is well wooded and remains so almost to Alton village where it becomes shallower. This section is perhaps the prettiest part of the valley, but it is often neglected by visitors to the Peak District. The reason for this is the lack of roads which keep the motorcar away. It is still traversed by its railway and canal and the latter adds much to the tranquil atmosphere.

The valley of the River Dane is similar to the Churnet in that motor traffic is denied access to much of it. The river rises on Axe Edge above Three Shires Head and flows roughly westwards to the Cheshire plain where it meanders slowly towards the River Weaver. It has a tributary, the Clough Brook which collects the waters from the Wildboarclough district. The brook is not of any importance but it does give us another large and beautiful dale to explore.

The valleys of the Dane and Clough Brook were important to the laden packhorses which crossed the southern Pennines carrying salt to the east of England. An interesting feature of Three Shires Head — where the counties of Cheshire, Derbyshire and Staffordshire meet — are the many packhorse routes which converge on Panniers Pool Bridge. This is an old packhorse bridge, now the exclusive preserve of the rambler.

Lower downstream near Gradbach a huge landslip has created a gorge of considerable proportions high on the hillside. It is known as Lud Church and is well worth the effort of getting to it. In excess of fifty feet high and in places only a few feet wide, it became a meeting place of religious dissenters some 500 years ago and supposedly takes its name from their leader. Above Lud Church and Back Forest in which it is situated, various paths cut through the heather and bilberry amid the exposed gritstone rock. This is the home of the grouse, curlew and, believe it or not, a small colony of wallabies, which were once part of a private zoo on the Roaches, but there are probably now only about six animals and so one has to be lucky to find them. Below Dane Bridge, where a

road crosses the valley and makes a good starting place to explore the area, the valley is the preserve of the rambler again. After a few miles it widens out and ends abruptly under the shadow of Bosley Cloud, a huge outcrop of harder gritstones.

The Goyt starts close to the Dane in the wide expanse of peat bogs north of Three Shires Head. Once the tree line is reached the valley becomes of more interest but its physical character is lost beneath the waters of Fernilee and Errwood reservoirs. To the west rises Shining Tor and the exposed edge of gritstone known as Windgather Rocks. There is however much of interest despite being flooded.

Historical Connections

Compared with other areas of the Peak, there is not a great deal remaining of early occupation in this area. A notable exception is the prehistoric burial mound known as the Bridestones, situated at the southern end of the large hill known as Bosley Cloud close to the Congleton-Rushton-Leek road. It is a chambered burial with some very tall standing stones. It is visible from the road, accessible to the public and well worth examining. The road which passes it is part of the Earls Way — an old route from the Earl of Chester's land in Cheshire to the Dieulacresse abbey at Leek (founded by an Earl of Chester) and his properties east of the town — and is at least medieval in origin. While parked by the Bridestones, look out to the west. On a clear day one can see the Welsh Hills and much nearer, Jodrell Bank Radio Telescope.

Dieulacresse Abbey at Leek has been completely destroyed, except for a small part of a pillar and is in any case on private ground, but of comparable age is the town's parish church which is well worth a visit. It is perhaps worthy of note that the roof of the abbey church was re-erected on the walls of Gasworth Church near Macclesfield and can still be seen. The parish church of St Edward the Confessor at Leek is on a very ancient site for it was founded in 1042. It has a beautiful pair of thirteenth-century rose windows; a ducking stool and ancient crosses in the churchyard. Despite alterations over a thousand years much of interest remains of the old church. A guide book is on sale at the church.

Two further churches of similar age to Leek are Cheddleton and Horton, situated about four miles south and west of Leek respectively. Further north Rushton church, chiefly built of stone and wood and situated in the fields halfway between Rushton James and Rushton Spencer to serve both villages, is well worth a visit. Two further churches are noteworthy, North of Wildboarclough is Forest Chapel erected in 1673 and rebuilt in 1834, where the annual rush laying ceremony can be observed. The other is the Roman Catholic Church at Cheadle, Staffordshire, which was built during 1840-6 and is considered to be the finest Victorian Gothic church in the country. It was designed by A.W.N. Pugin while enjoying the patronage and friendship of the Earl of Shrewsbury who paid out some £40,000 for it. It is incongruously situated off the main street, its huge spire over-shadowing the town. But its richly painted interior is a not-to-be-over-looked 'must' for many visitors.

There are several houses of considerable antiquity in the district. Most are not open to the public, but in some cases a footpath passes quite near. For instance, there are Whitehough and Sharpcliffe Hall between Leek and Ipstones, Wincle Grange near Wincle, the remains of the Norman castle near Alton, Alton Towers and the delightful Gawsworth Hall (open daily, April-October).

The Churnet Valley

The water of the valley gave rise to textile industries which developed to take advantage of its power and purity. Both Leek and Macclesfield developed as textile towns, but from the visitors point of view, while Macclesfield has a much better shopping centre, Leek is more interesting. The pure water of the Churnet gave rises to the development of the dyeing industry. This grew particularly in the nineteenth century when it was found that the water could be used to produce the raven-black dyes for which the town became so famous and which were so popular with the Victorians. Old textile mills mingle with silk workers' houses, but none are open to the public, although various 'mill shops' sell garments; slacks, ladies nightwear and underwear etc.

A walk around Leek's main streets reveals the Victorian influence particularly under the design of a local firm of architects. The town's cornmill in Mill Street has been preserved and is worth a visit. Although claimed by the enthusiasts to have been built by James Brindley, there is actually little proof of this, despite the fact that he had his workshops in the town. The waterwheel and all its machinery are intact and in working condition and the second floor has been developed as a museum to Brindley. Although better known as a canal engineer, his early career was as a millwright and he had close ties with the town.

An interesting phenomenom is sometimes observed from the churchyard on 20-22 June inclusive each year. At this time, if conditions are satisfactory, the setting sun can be seen

Staffordshire Art and Craft Centre
Craft shop and restaurant situated in former school at Cauldon Lowe. Exhibitions featured regularly.

Alton Towers
Built in the early years of the nineteenth century as the home of the Earls of Shrewsbury. This vast mansion is now a shell but the building is open to visitors. The gardens are well worth a visit — the whole head of the valley was converted into a magnificent showpiece. A leisure park has also been built along the lines of Disneyland. It is now the third most popular tourist attraction in Britain.

Alton village
Although now a fashionable commuter village, the old Norman castle remains still survive. Look for the village lock up, and the castle, rebuilt by Pugin. Down in the valley bottom the old mill, Italianate railway station and Lodge to Alton Towers are situated close together. The valley road to Oakamoor, hugging the river and enveloped in wooded glades is very attractive. The road back to Alton via Farley is worth taking. Look for the delightful hall in Farley village.

Hazelhurst Locks
Situated near to Denford south-west of Leek on the Caldon Canal. Here the Leek and Froghall branches of the canal join. The area often features in Inland Waterways Board publicity photographs. It is approached along the towpath from Denford. 'Staircase' locks, a canal aqueduct and a lock-keeper's cottage.

Froghall Wharf
A picnic site at a former canal-railway loading area. Fascinating industrial archaeology: canal basin, warehouse, railway trans-shipment area, limekilns, tramway inclines and a base for a number of interesting walks. Canal trips by horse-drawn narrow boat and a restaurant in the old warehouse.

Consall Forge
A major beauty spot on the western side of the Peak District. It has the advantage of being car free and therefore the number of visitors is not as great as in other areas. It may be approached along the canal from Cheddleton and Froghall or by footpath from Consall or Belmont. The Churnet Valley from Cheddleton to Froghall may be explored along the canal towpath.

to set behind Bosley Cloud completely, only to re-appear and finally set over the Cheshire plain. The double sunset can never be guaranteed, but many go to watch this spectacle each year.

Nearby, at Cheddleton on the A520 south of Leek, is a preserved flint mill.

The picturesque site is adjacent to the Caldon Canal and a preserved narrow boat is moored here. Flint stones were calcined in kilns and ground to powder and then used in the Potteries to make bone china, hence its local importance. There are two water-wheels and the mill

Cheddleton Flint Mill

has become an important tourist attraction, where the whole process is demonstrated and can be seen.

Although one can no longer travel by British Rail in this immediate vicinity, two steam railway centres have been established. While at Cheddleton, the old railway station about a mile downstream can be visited. It has a small collection of rolling stock and a museum devoted to the North Staffordshire Railway has been established. A little further south at the Foxfield Light Railway near to Dilhorne, just off the Cheadle to Stoke-on-Trent road, you can take a ride on a steam train for a few miles along a restored colliery line.

It has already been indicated that there are many beauty spots in the Churnet Valley but quite a few do demand that you leave the car behind. Furthermore the lack of roads down the valleys, a feature particularly pertinent

in the Churnet and Dane, does mean exploring both sides separately.

The main appeal of the Churnet lies below Cheddleton, where the valley bottom can be followed along the canal towpath to Froghall and rewards the effort. If you are particularly interested in canals and their architecture, take your car to Denford, just off the Leek to Hanley road (A53) at Longsdon. Walk westwards past the canalside pub (The Hollybush) under the aqueduct which carries the Leek arm of the canal, to Hazelhurst locks, where the Froghall branch locks down. There is a canal keeper's cottage, a rather nice cast-iron footbridge and much to interest the photographer.

The Cheddlton to Froghall section really starts at Basford Bridge near the railway station. The valley is well wooded and the leafy glades provide a marvellous backcloth for the canal.

Consall Forge is a small hamlet on the canal, with no public road to it, only a private estate road. Steep steps descend from each side of the valley to reach it, giving a more direct access than along the canal towpath. The hamlet gets its name from an old iron forge which existed in Elizabethan times, but all trace of it has long gone. Here, the canal and river run in one channel — a broad expanse of slow moving water which separates again in front of the old canal pub — the Black Lion, now the preserve of ramblers and pleasure boat users. The canal disappears under a footbridge and the railway to meander casually down to Froghall and the wharf there. The river commences its own course once more at the foot of a large weir and the whole scene is worth stopping to examine and photograph. Look out also for the remains of the huge lime kilns near to the canal. The railway no longer carries passengers, just sand from Oakamoor to St Helens in Lancashire.

Below Consall Forge is Podmore's Flint Mill, the sole surviving and still commercially operated local flint crushing mill serving the pottery industry. It is still using water power — but turbines and not water wheels, which have been removed. Two to three miles further on is Froghall with its vast copper works and canal wharf. Here a picnic area has been created at the canal basin, and one can explore the limekilns and loading docks where limestone was loaded onto railway wagons or into narrow boats. The quarry wagons ran on a 3ft 6in gauge track and lengths of rail of this gauge remain. With the 2ft 6in gauge of the Manifold Valley Light Railway, the North Stafford Railway was the only railway company in Britain to have lines of three different gauges. The incline to the quarry at Cauldon Lowe was the second oldest in the country, dating from 1777. If you are in Froghall with a car, take the Kingsley road and turn right along a narrow lane which gives several views down into the valley and is particularly useful if time does not permit a walk. It eventually passes a footpath marked 'Consull'. A quarter of a mile walk down here gives further excellent views into the valley and access to the canal towpath at Podmore's flint mill.

PLACES OF INTEREST AROUND THE CHURNET VALLEY

Croxdon Abbey
Large scale remains of Cistercian Abbey at Croxdon near Rocester and Alton. In the care of the Department of the Environment and open to the public.

JCB Factory, Rocester
Large excavator works in a rural setting with large scale use of water for landscaping. Introduced colony of various species of waterfowl best seen from the road to Hollington.

Cheadle RC Church
Accredited as being the finest example of Victorian Gothic architecture, built during 1840-6 to the design of A.W.N. Pugin. Richly decorated interior.

Foxfield Light Railway, Dilhorne, Cheadle.
Steam trains on 3 miles of private line, which was formerly used as a branch line to Foxfield Colliery. There is also a static display of other locomotives.

Coombes Valley Nature Reserve
Situated at SK010534 just off the Leek to Ashbourne road near to Apesford at Six Oaks Farm.

Hawkesmore Nature Reserve
Situated at Greenhill on the Cheadle to Oakamoor road. Three trails through the wooded side of the Churnet Valley.

The valley between Froghall and Oakamoor is denied even to the rambler but the latter village is worth investigation. It has two old pubs and a picnic site on the foundations of an old copper works, demolished in 1963 and now consolidated at Froghall. Here Messrs T. Bolton & Sons manufactured the copper wire core for the first transatlantic cable in 1856. Other than a few date stones, nothing now remains of the mill except for a very large mill pool, the retained water cascading down a stepped weir before disappearing under the road bridge. Within a short walking distance is Cotton Dell, which is well wooded and quite attractive. A path leaves the B5417 at GR057450 and crosses the Dell, which is private. It leaves Star Wood to rejoin the Whiston road above Oakamoor.

The section of valley between Oakamoor and Alton offers an alternative. The road via Farley leaves the valley, affording views of the latter and the Weaver Hills. It goes through Farley village with its attractive cottages and beautiful hall, once the home of the Bill family. Beyond Farley, the views are towards Alton Towers, its turrets soaring above the trees. The more direct route to Alton keeps to the valley bottom. The road is narrow but rewards patience in summer months. On reaching the Pink Lodge, walk westwards up Dimmings Dale to its old mill and the beautiful pools beyond. Alton village once enjoyed the patronage of the Earls of Shrewsbury who owned almost everything in the area. Look out for the village lock-up and the castle. The valley bottom at Alton has much to offer. The view up to the castle, perched high on the rocks looks like a Rhineland replica. The old railway station, built by A.W.N. Pugin, has been restored, while opposite is an

Dimmings Dale

old watermill. It is difficult to imagine that this old mill was once a copper and brass wire mill, producing 'Guinea-rods' in huge quantities as currency for the slave trade. Look out also for the lodge to the Towers, also attributed to Pugin.

An important tourist attraction in this south-western region is the former home of the Earls of Shrewsbury, Alton Towers. This huge mansion is situated near to Alton village in the Churnet Valley. Today the great house is a gutted shell, but the grounds have been developed as a leisure park, with many attractions for young and old, including its famous 'corkscrew' which loops twice. Over the last few years, the grounds have been developed into a massive leisure park on the Disneyland theme. The gardens were once billed as the largest domestice gardens in Europe. Now Alton Towers is billed as Europe's premier leisure park with over sixty

rides, shows and other attractions, including the world's largest log flume (800 metres in length), a circus, two cineramas and many others for all ages. The contrasts seem endless: rides for small children and rides that look terrifying; the delightfully situated licensed restaurant in the Swiss Cottage overlooking the garden and the Talbot Restaurant, the largest fast-food restaurant in Europe; peace and quiet in the gardens and ruins of the house and just the opposite in the theme areas of Fantasy World, Festival Park and Aqualand.

Of particular interest are the gardens, where hundreds of workmen toiled to convert a whole valley into a magnificent garden. It gained its effect by 'impressiveness of sheer profusion' as one writer put it. Around the valley are many paths and steps and one can find a corkscrew fountain, a Gothic temple, a

three storey 'Stone Henge', a Swiss
chalet, a huge range of conservatories
and much use of water. In the summer
one can often hear a band playing in the
bandstand and over the tree tops, see
water shooting into the sky from a
'Chinese Pagoda' fountain, its gold
painted bells glistening through the
falling water, There is much to see here
and although at first glance it appears
not to be cheap to gain admittance for
the family, it is well worth going for a
whole day. Alton Towers is a big place
attracting big crowds. You may prefer to
make your visit mid-week when there
are less people about and less queuing
for attractions. The gardens are
particularly worth seeing in the spring
when the rhododendrons are in flower.
At this time of year you can really
appreciate what 'impressiveness of sheer
profusion' really means.

The Dane Valley and Upper Goyt
The Dane Valley with its tributary the
Clough Brook rivals the Churnet and

*The Chinese Pagoda Fountain, Alton
Towers*

Talbot Street, Alton Towers

20

Three Shires Head

Dove Valleys as a major beauty spot in the west of the Peak District. Rising on Whetstone Edge, close to the Cat and Fiddle Inn, its deeply cut valley confines the infant waters of the river. Using old packhorse routes as paths it is possible to walk down much of the valley. The old bridge at Three Shires Head should

The 'Winking Eye', The Roaches

Gun Hill

Situated between Rushton and Meerbrook is the heather covered dome of Gun Hill. It is a good vantage point for viewing Tittesworth Reservoir, and on a clear day, the Wrekin, the Welsh Hills and the Jodrell Bank radio telescope.

The Roaches and Ramshaw Rocks

If you are travelling from Leek towards Buxton beneath Ramshaw Rocks, look for the 'Winking Eye' rock looking like a face. Watch its 'eye' and wait for it to wink at you! The Roaches are now owned by the Peak Park Planning Board. There are several footpaths which allow the gritstone escarpments to be discovered, along with some of the best walking country in Staffordshire.

Brindley Mill, Mill Street, Leek

A restored water driven cornmill and a display devoted to James Brindley, who had connections with the town.

Morridge

The views are considerable from Morridge for it not only looks down on the Roaches but also across to the Welsh Hills and the Wrekin. The Mermaid Inn is an old drovers' inn, still selling good beer and food, just across from the Gliding Club.

North Staffordshire Steam Railway Centre, Cheddleton Station, Nr Leek

A steam railway museum centred on the old Cheddleton Railway Station and dedicated to the North Staffordshire Railway Company. Although it has a locomotive in steam, there is only a limited amount of track available.

Cheddleton Flint Mill, Cheddleton, Nr Leek

Situated by the canal and river Churnet, this old flint mill has been restored and operates every weekend. In addition to flint grinding machinery there is also a narrow boat preserved on the canal at the side of the site.

not be missed. Have a look underneath it to see that the bridge has been widened at some time in the past. It is now hard to imagine that the amount of horse traffic was once so great as to necessitate the widening of this remote and disused bridge.

This may be the case, but alternatively the widening could have been for the passage of carts. It brings to mind Coldwall bridge on the Dove between Thorpe and Blore — a massively embanked turnpike bridge which is now disused and largely forgotten.

A couple of miles downstream from the bridge is Gradbach, a scattered community with no village as such. It is easily approached off the A53, the Leek to Buxton road, through Flash, the highest village in England. It is a harsh village of weather worn cottages, huddled together on the side of Oliver Hill. Descending down to the Dane, the scenery is more interesting and the climate more tolerant. Gradbach is worth taking time to explore. Not having a village centre, it is best to leave the car where the road is wide enough to permit this. Look for the old Methodist Chapel, built in 1849, and the adjacent cottage by the bridge over the river before walking downstream towards Gradbach Mill and Back Forest. It is easy to find, simply take the road to Flash from the bridge and turn first right down the side of a small brook. It is however a narrow road and it is better to walk than take the car.

Gradbach Mill is now owned by the Youth Hostels Association, but used to be a silk mill with a large waterwheel fed by water from the Dane. It was rebuilt in 1758 following a fire, and closed down

---

PLACES OF INTEREST IN THE DANE AND GOYT VALLEYS

Three Shires Head
Several old packhorse routes, now footpaths, make for the old bridge situated where Staffordshire meets Cheshire and Derbyshire. It is now a quiet beauty spot, the preserve of the rambler, curlew and grouse, and a fascinating place to explore. This is a far cry from the packhorse days for the bridge had to be widened to cope with the traffic using it.

Clough Brook
The valley of the Clough brook from Allgreave, north of Wincle, up to Wildboarclough and north to Bottom-of-the-Oven, can be seen from the car and rewards investigation.

Flash
The highest village in England with two of the highest pubs in England within its parish, plus footpaths to the Dane Valley and Three Shires Head.

The Cat and Fiddle Inn
Situated on the A537, the Buxton to Macclesfield road, at a height of 1,690ft above sea level. It is the highest inn in England with a full licence. From here there are some bracing walks to the Goyt Valley or over to Dane Bower and Wildboarclough

Gradbach
Despite narrow roads and few good parking areas, Gradbach is a further base for exploration of the Dane, particularly the Back Forest, Roach End and Ludchurch area. Gradbach Mill is now a Youth Hostel.

Danebridge
This small hamlet on the Dane is a useful base to explore the Dane Valley, either towards Back Forest or downstream to Gig Hall Bridge. It has a trout farm where you can buy fresh trout or fish for the day if you prefer a day's angling. A footpath starts downstream from close to Danebridge. This leads to a large weir across the river after about a mile. Here starts the feeder channel to Rudyard Reservoir which may be followed down river or all the way to the reservoir.

Goyt Valley
The twin reservoirs of Errwood and Fernilee now occupy much of this valley but the ruins of Errwood Hall remain and the yachts add much to the area's tranquillity. Many of the old hall's rhododendron survive and are worth seeing in summer. In the grounds of the hall, on the western side of Errwood reservoir is the Errwood Trail.

as a silk mill about 100 years later. Its large waterwheel was scrapped in the 1950s. A good example of an old packhorse road can be seen ascending the hill on the opposite side of the river from the mill. Below the mill lies Lud Church and Back Forest which was stripped of its main timber about twenty eight years ago. Lud Church has already been mentioned but it is worth repeating that it repays a visit, preferably on a walk from Gradbach around by Hanging Stone to Danebridge and Swythamley. Much of the area south of the river between Gradbach and Danebridge formed part of the Swythamley Estate which was divided and sold in lots in 1977. The estate also included Swythamley Hall, now a transcendental centre, plus the Roaches which where purchased in 1980 by the Peak Park Planning Board in a deal costing £185,000.

If the walk mentioned above is taken, stop near the Hanging Stone. The view over Swythamley and south eastwards towards the Roaches is worth more than a passing glance. Indeed before coming over the bluff from Gradbach the view northwards up to the Clough Brook

Gradbach Mill

24

The Roaches: Hen Cloud with Five Clouds behind

with the high hill of Shutlingsloe rising to 1,659ft is even more interesting. The Hanging Stone carries two plaques, one to the brother of the last Brocklehurst of Swythamley. He was Lt Col Brocklehurst, who had been a gamewarden in the Sudan, and who established a private zoo on the Roaches which included deer, a kangaroo, wallabies and a yak. Descendants of the deer and wallabies still roam these hills. The other plaque is to a pet dog. Upon reaching Danebridge take the well defined path back to Gradbach through the fields above the river Dane. The path starts by the side of the bridge at Danebridge.

Further north under the hill of Shutlingsloe lies Wildboarclough. Taking the road westwards from Gradbach, a couple miles brings one to Allgreave where the minor road joins the A54. Just beyond the Clough Brook a minor road turns off to the right to run northwards towards Shutlingsloe. This road hugs the brook all the way to Wildboarclough. It is an attractive route and passes the Crag Inn, a popular stopping off place for visitors. The village boasted the largest sub post office in England before it closed. This distinction arises from the post office being in what was the administration block of an old textile mill, now demolished. Traces of it can be seen from the road at the T junction just up river from the Crag Inn. On the hillside above the post office is Crag Hall, the country seat of Lord Derby. The roadway near to the hall abounds with rhododendrons which are a riot of colour in the summer. If time permits, continue upstream for half a mile or so and leave the car where the signpost indicates the path to Cumberland Clough. Walk up the brook past the deep ravine with its rushing white water, rugged and dark conifers, to the waterfall before returning to the car

Just above Danebridge the waters of the Clough and Dane unite to form a good sized river flowing beneath the

1¼m

broad arch after which the village takes its name. Like many neighbouring communties, Danebridge consists of a few loosely grouped cottages. It also has an interesting old pub, the Ship Inn, with some interesting relics of the 1745 uprising including a flintlock of a Scottish soldier and part of a newspaper he was carrying. The name Ship Inn, is said to be a reminder of the SS *Swithamley (sic)*, although the present inn sign is of the *Nimrod* which took Shackleton, and Sir Phillip Brocklehurst of Swythamley, to the Antarctic.

The broad fields below Danebridge, broken by areas of woodland and views of Bosley Cloud make a pleasant walk to Gig Hall Bridge where the feeder channel to Rudyard reservoir starts. Above the valley is Wincle Grange Farm where the monks of old had a sheep and cattle farm. Further north, and connected by a track to the Grange is Cleulow Cross, now hidden by the trees which surround it. It probably was a waymark cross on the route to the coast from Dieulacresse Abbey at Leek, which had important holdings of sheep and is known to have exported wool to Italy. Nearby is the modern and incongruous (but very necessary) radio telegraphy mast of British Telecom, one of the chain which stretches from British Telecom tower near Euston Station in London.

From Gig Hall Bridge, the feeder supply winds down the valley to Rushton. It has a path at the side, much in the nature of a towpath, which provides a pleasant walk. Below the village lies Rudyard Lake. It was built by John Rennie as a water supply to the Trent and Mersey Canal and today is a popular resort for yachtsmen and fishermen alike.

North of the Dane lies Macclesfield Forest, the high moorland of Shining Tor and the Goyt. The road upstream from Wildboarclough can be used as a good introduction to the area. Turn first left (above the village, opposite Dryknowle Farm). The road soon enters the forest to pass between Trentabank and Ridgegate Reservoirs. Upon reaching the road junction opposite the pub turn right up the narrow road which climbs steeply uphill. A deviation to the left and into Tegg's Nose Country Park may be made if time permits. The narrow road climbs up to the hamlet of Macclesfield Forest with its little, rugged chapel and school. Continue to Bottom-of-the-Oven and then drive up the lane northwards to Lamaload reservoir. It has a picnic area at its northern end but a better stopping place is a Errwood Reservoir.

From Lamaload, proceed to Jenkin Chapel erected in 1733 at John Slack's expense as a tablet records. Turn eastwards and climb over Pym Chair before dropping down to the twin reservoirs of Errwood and Fernilee.The former rivals Rudyard with its yachts and there is a picnic site overlooking the water. A detour to the ruins of Errwood Hall near the south-western end of the water is an interesting diversion, particularly when the rhododendrons are in bloom. Leave the Goyt after crossing the dam. The steep inclined road was formerly part of the Cromford and High Peak Railway and wagons used to be hauled up the incline by a steam engine at the top. This is the reason for the reservoir at the top of the incline — it provided water for the steam engine's boiler.

Outdoor Activities

In addition to the many walks, there are a variety of outdoor pursuits available. The Roaches and Windgather Rocks have been used by climbers for a long

The ruins of Errwood Hall, Goyt Valley

time and the recent purchase of the former by the Peak Park Planning Board has secured access to the rock faces, which are numerous, with various grades of severity.

Canoeing is also becoming very popular on the Caldon Canal and enables one to see the beauty of the valley from a different angle. Alternatively, if you are not so adventurous, narrow boat trips on the canal from Froghall and Cheddleton are now available.

Visitors are welcome at the Coombes Valley Nature Reserve, which protects woodland and pasture in the Coombes Valley, a tributary of the Churnet, between Cheddleton and Ipstones near to Leek. The Hawkesmore Nature Reserve near Oakamoor, on the road to Cheadle also welcomes visitors and a trail has been laid out in the extensive grounds under its ownership, which drop towards the Churnet.

For the more adventurous, the Staffordshire Gliding Club which has its headquarters on Morridge near Leek, adjacent to the Mermaid Inn, is prepared to take you up for a fee to give you a unique view of the area you are exploring.

Other Walks

There are a variety of walks in this area which enable one to really see the area at its best, particularly as the beauty spots are, for the most part, denied to the motorist. In the Churnet Valley the canal towpath from Froghall, where there is a picnic centre, can be used to gain access to Consall Forge. Alternatively there are two paths which descend more directly to the hamlet. The towpath from Froghall, as distinct from Cheddleton which can be muddy, is useful for pushing wheelchairs, although there is a bridge with steps to cross.

The more direct paths descend to the Churnet from Consall village and from Belmont. In each case there are numerous steps to descend but Consall Forge is well worth the effort. Park in Consall village and walk eastwards towards the valley. At a bend in the road, a signpost to Consall Forge indicates the start of a well used path which crosses the fields before descending down into the valley.

The more interesting route to the river is from Belmont pools, down the 'Devil's Staircase'. The 200 steps bring one down from the wood near to Belmont pools through the estate of Belmont Hall (which is not open to the public). The car may be parked at Belmont pools on the Cheddleton to Ipstones road and the path (not the hall drive) taken to Consall Forge. The pools have long been popular for photographic studies — the huge beech trees create an almost perfect setting for the artifical pools. By the road here is an old chapel with its small tower and east window. It did not have a religious use for long and was built when the owner of the hall fell out with the vicar of Ipstones. It has recently been carefully restored but again it is a private residence and is not open to the public.

The area around Three Shires Head has several old packhorse routes which can be used for exploring. The one from Flash Bar via Drystone Edge and Blackclough can be used for wheelchairs, if you do not mind the path being a little rough in places. It has a tarmac or stone surface for much of its

---

PLACES OF INTEREST AROUND LEEK

Church of Edward the Confessor
Known in Leek as 'The old church', it stands adjacent to the market place. Much of the fabric dates from 1297. It has two rose-windows, several crosses or cross fragments, a ducking stool, etc.

From the churchyard a 'double sunset' may be seen on 20-22 June if climatic conditions are right. In the churchyard on the slopes on the north side of the church are many graves of French officers of the Napoleonic wars.

Rudyard Lake
Built by John Rennie as a water supply to the Trent and Mersey Canal system. It is now very popular for yachts and angling. Boats may be hired from the dam end. You can also walk around it.

Deep Haye Country Park
A former reservoir reduced in size because of doubts about the long-term stability of the dam wall and converted into a country park.

Bridestones and Bosley Cloud
Large escarpment with extensive views across the Cheshire Plain and over into the Peak District. The Bridestones is a chambered burial tomb of prehistoric age with some very tall standing stones. It is situated close to the Congleton to Rushton road and south-east of Timbersbrook village.

Tittesworth Reservoir
Large reservoir on the River Churnet just south of the Roaches. Angling is available, plus a picnic area at the northern end, near to Meerbrook

way but is not open to motor vehicles. Further down the Dane, the path from Danebridge to Gradbach, to include Ludchurch, is worth considering together with the path downstream from Danebridge at least as far as the start of the feeder supply to Rudyard Lake, at Gig Hall Bridge.

A good circular route, taking in the Dane and Clough Brook is recommended. For convenience, start at Wildboarclough where there is adequate roadside car parking. Just upstream of the Crag Inn take the footbridge over the brook and climb over the hill to the main road (A54) and Tagsclough Hill. From here, this old packhorse route continues straight to Gradbach Mill via Burntcliff Top. It emerges at the Flash to Allgreave road by the side of an old pub, the Eagle and Child, now a private house. Inside the entrance is a motif of an eagle and child taken from the arms of the Stanleys, Earls of Derby, who own Crag Hall and its estate at Wildboarclough. From Gradbach Mill proceed upstream to the chapel where a path cuts up the hill, east of the Dane to Turn Hill where it meets the packhorse route to Three Shires from Flash. Cross the bridge at Three Shires Head and continue over to Cumberland Clough via Holt Farm and the western edge of Dane Bower. Follow the clough down to the road and turn downstream to Wildboarclough.

North of the Dane, the upper Goyt down to Errwood reservoir makes a good walk, together with some time spent exploring the ruins of Errwood Hall and its gardens. Cars must be parked at Derbyshire Bridge, but on Sundays in summer a minibus is available to take you much nearer to Errwood. If you visit the area midweek and drive from the Pym Chair, or west side of the valley, you can drive down to Errwood and out via Derbyshire Bridge.

There are youth hostels at Dimmings Dale near to Oakamoor and at Meerbrook. A new hostel has been established at Gradbach at the old silk mill which enables one to explore the area easily.

PLACES OF INTEREST IN THE MACCLESFIELD AREA

Gawsworth Hall, 3m south of Macclesfield on the Congleton road. A sixteenth-century half-timbered manor house which was the home of the Fittons, including Mary Fitton, thought to be the Dark Lady of Shakespeare's Sonnets. In the grounds of the hall one of the last remaining tournment grounds in the country still survives. This is still a family home, steeped in history and well rewards a visit.

The roof at Gawsworth church came from Dieulacresse Abbey, Leek, after the dissolution of the monastry.

Macclesfield Canal
Runs south of the town, just to the west of the A523 road to Leek.

Teggs Nose Country Park
Situated north of Langley village west of Macclesfield Forest.

Lyme Hall and Park (National Trust), Disley, 6½m south-east of Stockport, Elizabethan house with eighteenth- and nineteenth-century additions, large deer park and gardens. Situated on the main road from Disley to Hazel Grove.

Events and Festivals

In addition to the activities mentioned above there are various events and festivals which are worth bearing in mind. Leek has an impressive gathering one Saturday in July, know as Club Day. Its basis is the gathering in the Market Place of the children from the town's Sunday Schools. It is, however, augmented by other groups and associations from within the town. After the singing of hymns and a few prayers, the procession leads off in a walk around the main streets. Lorries carrying little children are gaily decorated and the various old banners of the Sunday Schools are an impressive sight. The event is very popular and the streets on the route are usually packed with spectators.

Each August, Leek has its Agricultral Show on the flat playing fields opposite the Britannia Building Society Headquarters. This is quite a large affair with a full programme all day of both agricultural and non-agricultural activities. While also dealing with Leek, the 'double sunset' of June 20-22, should not be overlooked. Nearby, on the west side of Leek, lies the village of Endon. Now a dormitory for the Potteries and Leek, the old village celebrates its well dressing at Spring Bank Holiday. It too is quite a festival with thousands of visitors.

To the north, on the edge of Macclesfield Forest, lies the squat flagstone-roofed Forest Chapel. On the nearest Sunday to 12 August, the floor of the church is spread with rushes as part of the Annual Rush Bearing Service. A service is held at the church in the afternoon and attracts many visitors. This tradition is a relic of a custom which was once quite common and it is satisfying to see that these (now quaint) practices are still preserved.

2 The Dove and Manifold Valleys

General Description

Both the rivers Dove and Manifold rise on the grits and shales of Axe Edge, in close proxmity to each other and to the rivers Goyt, Dane and Wye which divide this bleak upland area into different watersheds. All these rivers flow down deeply cut incised courses contrasting with the shallow valley of the river Hamps, the main tributary of the Manifold. The infant Dove and Manifold both rise close to the Traveller's Rest Inn at Flash Bar some 7½ miles up the Buxton road out of Leek. The River Dove forms the county boundary between Derbyshire and Staffordshire and its source is in a small well close to the road, marked with intertwined initials of CC and IW — Charles Cotton and Izaak Walton. This is a replica of the monogram carved on the fishing house in Beresford Dale downstream, but was erected in 1851, many years after both men fished the waters of the river. The Manifold's source can also be seen from the road, just to the south of the inn. Starting in a shallow depression, it is deeply cut into the landscape before leaving the field in which it rises.

The upper reaches of both rivers are quite spectacular and can be viewed quite easily by taking the Hollinsclough road from the Traveller's Rest Inn. The inn itself enjoys quite a reputation for the large number of different draught

Crowdecote

31

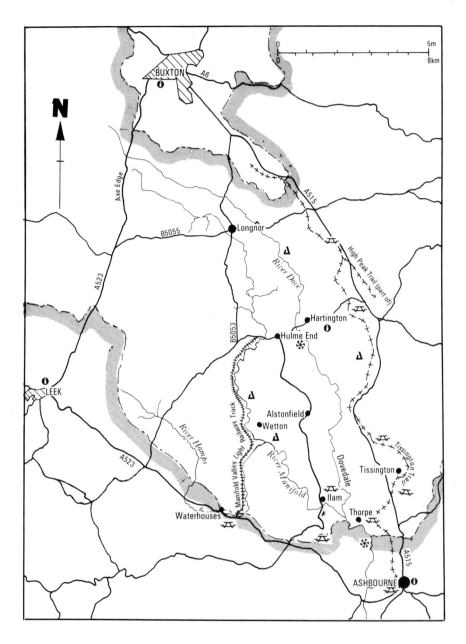

beers available at the bar. The road soon climbes Edge Top where one can pull off the road and view both valleys at the same time. At this point the Manifold has cut deeply into the gritstone formations but the more spectacular view is towards Hollinsclough and the hills beyond. It is here that the overlying grits are replaced by the older limestones. These are chiefly bedded but

Lyme Hall

Three Shires Head

Alton Towers

Washgate Bridge

a characteristic of this side of the limestone and gritstone boundary is the reef knolls which are in massive limestone, and have not yet yielded in the same way to the forces of erosion. The result is a succession of hills on the edge of the limestone plateau which stretch down the Dove and to a much lesser extent occur in the Manifold as well. Examples are Hollins Hill, Chrome Hill, Parkhouse Hill, High Wheeldon, Thorpe Cloud, Thor's Cliff; and they are the closest one gets to 'peaks' in the Peak District. The fossil content of these rocks is also much more varied: while the bedded rocks contain chiefly crinoids and brachiopods, sea lilies (which are animals and not plants) and bivalve shells, the reefs also contain a greater variety of fossils such as trilobites, corals and goniatities. However, try to obtain your samples from quarry spoil heaps; do not hammer

indiscriminately and without permission.

Beyond Hollinsclough, the character of the two valleys changes. The Dove flows through a very deep limestone valley past Crowdecote towards Hartington, while the Manifold, still flowing across the softer overlying shales, occupies a very broad and shallow valley. This difference can easily be seen by taking the Longnor to Sheen road, which runs along the rounded bluff between both rivers which are less than a mile apart at one point.

Below Hartington and Hulme End both rivers occupy gorge-like valleys cut deeply into the limestone. The broad valley of the Manifold suddenly ends in the huge limestone dome of Ecton Hill. Hereafter it is characterised by huge incised meanders that wind in an interlocking pattern down to Ilam where the two rivers unite. It is these

33

The Market Hall, Longnor

spectacular meanders which give the river its name. This creates an ever-changing subject for the eye and camera and as a result the scenery is more varied

than the Dove Valley and also more interesting until one reaches the Milldale to Thorpe Cloud section of the river. This is Dovedale — a majestic stretch of the valley now unfortunately suffering from over-use by ramblers. With its natural ashwoods, numerous towers of natural stone and features such as Reynard's Arch and the Watchbox near Ilam Rock, it has much to commend it. Much of Dovedale is protected by the National Trust and the dale forms the major part of the Derbyshire Dales National Reserve. While many people stop at Ilam Rock few glance down river to try and spot the Watchbox, a huge mass of stone perched high on the cliffs of the Derbyshire bank. It is supposed to be capable of being rocked by hand, but the author has never tried to prove whether this is true.

Between Ilam and Thorpe the two rivers unite. The Manifold is by far the larger river, but as the Dove is the county boundary it carries its name downstream from here until it reaches the river Trent near Burton. One of the main tributaries of these two rivers is the

Fields at Longnor, with Parkhouse Hill and Chrome Hill beyond

Coldwall Bridge over an abandoned coaching road near Thorpe

Hamps which flows off Morridge near to Leek and flows in a very broad valley to Waterhouses where it too reaches the limestone and enters a deeply incised valley like the Manifold. It twists and turns with almost monotonous regularity until it joins the Manifold beneath the huge cliffs of Beeston Tor, which was purchased by the National Trust in 1976. An unusual feature of both the Hamps and the Manifold is the disappearance of the water during dry spells. The Hamps is swallowed up at Waterhouses down solution cavities in the limestone known as 'swallets', or elsewhere in the Peak as 'shack-holes'. There are more swallets at Wettonmill on the Manifold (on private ground) and a second group can be seen from the road just below Wettonmill at Redhurst, just before the Wetton road begins to climb out of the valley. Both

rivers occupy different underground channels and do not appear to unite. Coloured dyes take some 22-24 hours to re-emerge at the boilholes in the grounds of Ilam Hall, close to the riverside path.

Clearly the deep valleys have had an influence on the distribution and location of the many small villages scattered throughout the area. The upper and less productive soils have resulted in scattered farmhouses rather than communities and Longnor is the only village of any size, growing at the junction of two turnpike roads in the eighteenth century. Elsewhere the villages are situated on the rolling plateau above the valleys, with the notable exceptions of Hartington and Ilam. Waterhouses assumed some importance with the coming of the Manifold Valley Light Railway although the railhead at Hulme End failed to

Darfur Bridge, Manifold Valley

develop, primarily because of the
economic unimportance of its existence.
The only towns of any size are outside
the area at Buxton, Leek (described in
other chapters) and Ashbourne, each
exerting some influence over parts of the
area, particularly Leek and Ashbourne
which have cattle markets.

Historical Connections

Settlement in the area can be traced back
to the Palaeolithic or Old Stone Age
period. Many of the caves in the valleys
have yielded evidence of early
occupation, chiefly for shelter, although
some such as Ossum's Cave at Wettonmill
are known to have been occupied at a
workshop for fashioning flints. Even the
large Thor's Cave was occupied at one
stage. Many of the finds of these

caves can be viewed in Buxton Museum,
while other finds from Thor's Cave now
form part of the Bateman Collection in
Sheffield Museum.

Many burials were made in the
numerous 'lows' or tumuli which are
scattered across the area, but chiefly east
of the river Manifold. Excavation of
these was undertaken by Thomas
Bateman, a nineteenth-century barrow-
digger. Victorian antiquarians are now
frowned upon as their techniques were
often crude and the results poorly
documented. Bateman was somewhat
better than most of his comtemporaries,
although he did open four burial
mounds (at Hurdlow, close to the Earl
Sterndale to Brierlow Bar road) in one
day!

Nearby in Dowel Dale is a cave

situated close to the road and just above Dowel Farm. Excavation of this cave also yielded a communal burial of late Neolithic (or New Stone Age) date. There were skeletons of ten people, ranging from a baby to an old man, interred in the cave. Excavation work continues annually by the Peakland Archaeological Society whose current project is at Fox Hole Cave on High Wheeldon. Excavation work here has yielded remains dating back to the Middle Stone Age.

The Bronze Age and Iron Age are represented in the area through cave and tumuli excavation. There are no hillforts in the area which characterise other parts of the Peak. The Bronze Age people used caves for shelter but buried their dead in barrows or mounds of earth which were raised over a grave or a cremation. A good example of a barrow can be seen adjacent to the road at the Liffs on the Hartington to Alsop road, east of Biggin Dale, just into the field at the top of the hill. Liffs Low contained a cist made of slabs of limestone and contained two sets of flint axes, flint spearheads, flint knives and flint arrow heads amongst other material.

The more recent history of the area shows little Roman influence, although the area was occupied and farmed by Romano-British settlers at the time. A Roman coin of Severius was found at Hulme End during excavations for a cottage but no Roman encampments were established in the area. A motte and bailey castle was established north of Hartington at Pilsbury in Norman times, but little is known about it and full details await excavation.

The caves of the Manifold have also yielded a further find of much interest. During excavation of St Bertram's Cave at Beeston Tor in 1924, forty-nine Anglo-Saxon silver pennies of about AD871-4 were recovered. In addition there were two silver brooches and three gold rings.

In the Middle Ages parts of the area became the property of various religious orders and a small level platform at Musden Grange near Ilam is the supposed remains of the monastic grange. Following the dissolution of the monasteries the lands passed into private ownership and thereafter much land was under the influence of such families as the Duke of Devonshire — particularly at Hartington, Ecton and

Beresford Dale

The Fishing Temple, Beresford Dale

Wetton. The oldest son of the Duke of Devonshire is in fact Lord Hartington. Other estates were those of the Harpur Crewes (who owned much land around Warslow, Longnor and Alstonfield) and the FitzHerberts at Tissington.

Historical and literary associations with the area are numerous — particularly as a result of the popularity of Dovedale. Byron and Dr Johnson for example were visitors to the dale; Jean Jacques Rousseau knew it during his exile at nearby Wootton Hall; William Morris and other pre-Raphaelites, plus Mark Twain, were visitors to Sir

Thomas Wardle at Swainsley in the Manifold Valley. Perhaps the greatest name associated with the Dove is that of Izaak Walton who used to stay with his close friend — who became his adopted son — Charles Cotton. Cotton owned Beresford Hall and the Dove flowed through his estate. Beresford Dale is one of the prettiest places on the whole of the river and it was here that Cotton built a fishing house, dated 1674, which still survives. Cotton added chapters to Walton's *Compleat Angler* in the 5th edition before Walton died, his fame assured. Cotton also owned Throwley Hall at one time, but both Beresford and Throwley Halls are no more. Only a prospect tower of perhaps Tudor origin survives at Beresford, but the ruins of Throwley can be seen from the Calton to Ilam road. The fishing house is on private land, but can be seen from the footpath as one approaches the trees at the north end of the dale from Hartington.

In the past, people of the area found work chiefly in agriculture and to a lesser extent in the extractive industries or small waterpowered mills. It is a pattern reflected in all parts of the Peak. There is not a great deal to see of these former activities although early enclosures around Calton and south-east of Longnor preserve the ancient strip pattern of cultivation in the narrow fields that survive. The insular nature of former village communities seems to be reflected at Butterton where the field walls are built almost as circles around the village. Narrow cultivation terraces — or lynchets — can be found quite frequently in the lower parts of the valleys. A particularly fine set can be seen near Throwley Hall from the Ilam to Throwley road, particularly when the early morning sun is low in the sky. The early strip field system is preserved very

well in the fields to the west of the Buxton-Ashbourne road, between the two turnings to Tissington.

Much of the stone for dry stone walls was quarried locally and many small quarries and limekilns can be found. There are several, for instance, in Hartington Dale between the village and its old railway station. It was quite common for a farmer to have his own limekiln to burn stone for his land. A good quality gritstone was even mined at Daisy Knoll Farm, Longnor, providing much of the building stone for the village.

There are also many mines in the area. In the millstone grit of Axe Edge, coal was mined, while lower downstream lead, copper and zinc ores were extracted, which yielded varying fortunes or losses for the miners. At Ecton near Warslow, various mines can be observed from the roads or footpaths, which yielded considerable quantities of copper ore. The main mine reached a total depth of over 1,400ft and made a considerable fortune for the Duke of Devonshire, its owner. It had an early example of a Boulton and Watt steam engine, an underground canal for haulage purposes and several other unusual features, including a waterwheel for pumping, situated deep underground.

The waters of the main streams have long been used for water power. There were medieval mills at Hartington and Ilam for instance. The cornmill at Lode Mill near Alstonfield and the sawmill at Longnor remain intact, while Brund Mill west of Sheen and Hartington Mill have been converted to delightful dwellinghouses. Some of the water mills have had a varied history. Brund Mill was built in 1760 as a cornmill, but in 1790 this fine building was converted into a cotton mill by Thomas Cantrell, who got into financial difficulties with it four years later. It ended its days grinding corn during the last war and slowly fell into disrepair before being tastefully converted to a dwelling and retaining much of the machinery. Thomas Cantrell also had a cotton mill in Hartington which was built about 1776 on the site of what is now Minton House. The little cottages opposite were probably for his workers; they bear the initial T & JC 1777.

Little industry has survived to the present day. Two notable exceptions are

PLACES OF INTEREST IN THE DOVE AND MANIFOLD VALLEYS

River Manifold Swallets
The delightful Manifold valley takes its name from the many deeply incised meanders which occur below Hulme End. The river Manifold completely disappears underground at Wetton Mill and at Redhurst Swallet. It may be viewed from the road at GR098557 disappearing into Redhurst Swallet. It re-appears in the grounds of Ilam Hall, a few miles downstream. The grounds are owned by the National Trust, and therefore the boil holes where the water re-appears can also be seen.

Manifold Valley Light Railway
When the line was built at the beginning of the century, the locos were copies of those built for the Barsi Light Railway in India. They had headlamps and cow catchers, although the latter were never used. Some of the railway buildings survive at Hulme End, but the engines and picturesque coaches have all been scrapped. The eight-mile long track-bed from Hulme End to Waterhouses is now a tarmac-covered footpath/road; there is a short tunnel at Swainsley. Some stretches are ideal for the disabled, although the gates on certain sections may preclude a wheelchair.

Thor's Cave
Just below Wetton Mill is situated Thor's Cave with its huge 60ft entrance situated some 250ft above the river. There is a stiff climb up to the entrance from the river and the cave itself is not very deep, but the view more than compensates for this.

Ilam Hall and Country Park
Delightful riverside setting of former Victorian Gothic hall. Much of the hall has been demolished but the riverside paths should not be missed. Look out for the resurging waters of the rivers Manifold and Hamps. The latter being slightly upstream of the former. The surviving part of the hall is a Youth Hostel. The church is worth a visit and contains much of interest, including two Anglo-Saxon crosses in the churchyard and a monument by Sir Frances Chantrey.

Beeston Tor
Situated at the junction of the rivers Manifold and Hamps is the large cliff of Beeston Tor with St Bertram's Cave, where a hoard of Saxon silver brooches and coins was found in 1924.

the Hartington Stilton Cheese Factory and the silica fire-brick works at Friden — both remnants of long established industries. Cheese was formerly made at Glutton Bridge north of Longnor and Derby cheese was made at Reapsmoor. Both these buildings survive, but the factory established in old mine buildings at Ecton in the 1920s closed in 1933 and all buildings there have been demolished. The Hartington factory, now owned by the Milk Marketing Board, makes Stilton cheese which is exported all around the world. The

Ecton Mines
Site of eighteenth-century copper mine, one of the largest in Europe at the time and also one of the richest. The mine's profits are reputed to have financed the building of the Crescent in Buxton. There are remains of workings and buildings, but little of interest to mineralogists.

The Traveller's Rest Inn, Flash Bar Flash
This inn is situated by the old Buxton to Leek turnpike at a height of 1540ft OD and is one of the highest pubs in England. It is well known for the dozens of different drinks available on draught.

Mill Dale
This small hamlet is situated by an old packhorse bridge across the River Dove. It was used by Izaak Walton and Charles Cotton and is referred to in the 5th addition of the *Compleat Angler* published in 1676. The bridge is mentioned in a dialogue between 'Piscator' and 'Viator' and is now known as Viator's Bridge. Mill Dale is the northern entrance into the four-mile section of the river known as Dovedale.

Reef Knolls
The Limestone reef knolls of the upper Dove Valley are quite pronounced in the form of several hills, such as Parkhouse Hill and Chrome Hill. They are worth photographing and are best viewed from vantage points around Longnor, Earl Sterndale or Crowdecote; there are no public footpaths to their summits. They are about as close as one gets to 'peaks' in the Peak District!

Hartington Village
This well known and very popular village has a number of shops that are useful for restocking with provisions. There is a bank (Nat West, open Friday only), petrol station, gift shops, cafés, hotel, post office and of course the Stilton cheese factory shop. In Beresford Dale, south of the village, Charles Cotton's fishing temple, built in 1674 may be glimpsed through the trees, across the River Dove.

Alstonfield Village
A further delightful village near to Hartington, with a good pub popular with ramblers, post office, gift shop and grocery shop. There are many interesting buildings, including the church, which has fine carved oak box pews and Charles Cotton's family pew.

Warslow Brook,
Manifold Valley

Friden works commenced extracting sand from local pits in 1892. These are unusual pockets found in the limestone and the deposits are still being worked by DSF Refractories Ltd, making bricks for furnace hearth linings.

Despite being so rural the area was served by three railway lines. The Buxton to Ashbourne line was the most recent, for work commenced as late as 1890. At Parsley Hay it joined the Cromford and High Peak Railway for a while before leaving the latter to enter Buxton. The Cromford and High Peak Railway was built much earlier and is discussed later.

Of more interest perhaps is the narrow gauge (30in) railway that ran down the Manifold Valley from Waterhouses to Hulme End. This railway opened in 1904 and ran for 30 years. The old station buildings (except the coach shed) still remain at Hulme End. It was an unusual railway, modelled on a narrow gauge line in India.

Towns and Villages

Ashbourne is of course the main town serving the area. It has much of interest and plenty of things to see. Primarily a market town, it retains many eighteenth-century buildings together with other much older buildings in its main streets, such as the Gingerbread Shop which is timber framed and considered to be fifteenth century. It is probable that the town was originally situated further to the west and nearer the church which is

Ashbourne church

now almost out of the town, but
development of a new centre, including
the market place, probably began as
early as the thirteenth century. Places to
look out for in the town include the
Green Man and Black's Head Royal
Hotel. Its inn sign stretches over the
street as it is the longest hotel name in
the country, and it has a small courtyard
where coaches unloaded. Look at the
Black's Head carved on the inn sign; on
one side he smiles, on the other he is sad.
The inn which is of Georgian origin, has
associations with Boswell, who along
with Dr Johnson, stayed in the town
with a Dr Taylor who owned the

Mansion in Church Street.
   A walk along the street towards the
church is very rewarding. There are
many Georgian houses of interest
including No 61 The Grey House, which
is next to the Old Grammar School.
Pevsner describes Church Street as one
of the finest streets in Derbyshire. The
Grammar School was founded in 1585.
The central portion with four gables
above was the old schoolroom and the
schoolmaster's accommodation was at
either side, while opposite is The
Mansion with the almshouses built in
1614-30 adjacent.
   While in the street, visit the church,

Tissington Well Dressing

A visit to this village on, or just after Ascension Day, to see the annual well dressing ceremony should not be missed if at all possible. Using petals and other natural materials such as moss, pressed into clay set in a wooden frame, the five wells are 'dressed' to depict a particular religious theme. It is supposed to have originated from a desire to give thanksgivings for the ceaseless supply of pure water. Other well-dressings are listed in the 'Further Information'.

Carsington Reservoir

Situated south of Carsington and Hopton villages. It was intended that water collection for this new reservoir would begin in 1986 and a picnic area has already been laid out. The dam wall collapsed in June 1984 and at the time of writing the incident is under investigation. It seems unlikely that the project will proceed on schedule.

Rescue digs in the area proposed to be flooded have revealed substantial Roman remains, which may be the site of *Lutudarum,* the Roman's lead mining and smelting centre in the Peak District.

Tissington Trail

The former site of Hartington railway station is now a picnic site with toilet facilities and an information centre in the old signal box. The latter still retains its old lever frames and there are several photographs on the wall showing what the railway used to look like. The trail gives level walking and cycling north from Ashbourne. Cycles may be hired from the Peak Park Planning Board at Parsley Hay Wharf (SK147636) and Ashbourne (SK175470). If you hire a cycle from Parsley Hay and end up in Hartington, return via Long Dale, as it is a much easier gradient. Proceed eastwards out of the village, past the school and take the first turn to the left, into Long Dale.

Fenny Bentley

In the church is a curious tomb to Thomas Beresford who fought at Agincourt. The effigies of both Thomas and his wife are depicted bundled up in shrouds, as are their twenty-one children around the tomb. The tower of their fortified and moated manor house, may be seen from the A515 Ashbourne to Buxton road, or from the footpath which passes close by.

one of the grandest in the Peak, preferably in early spring when the churchyard is submerged beneath a delightful carpet of daffodils. The oldest part of the existing buildings dates from the thirteenth century although a Norman crypt has been located. The alabaster monuments in the church are especially notable, as well as a fine carving in marble of Penelope Boothby. There is a church guide book available. If you have time to spend exploring Ashbourne further — and it is well worth it — a Local History Trail written by the Arkwright Society is available at the book shop next to the National Westminster Bank.

Ashbourne is famed for its Shrovetide

Ashbourne

football match which occurs on Shrove
Tuesday and Ash Wednesday. The ball
is thrown up at 2.00pm in Shaw Croft
car park behind the Green Man Inn and
the game continues until nightfall. The
ball, made of leather filled with cork, is
thrown up by a personality with
Ashbourne connections. The goals are
three miles apart, on the site of the old
Clifton and Sturston Mills and teams,
consisting of hundreds, are known as the
'Up'ards' and 'Down'ards'. The rules
are few and the town shops are boarded
up to withstand the seige, for the 'hug' as
it is known, is no respecter of property;
even the river is part of the game. It is
the object of each team to get the ball
back to one's own goal, It is a slow-
moving game and it is rare for more than
one goal to be scored in a day's play.

In Ashbourne's St John's Street
behind an unprententious facade is Fosters

fishing tackle shop. Established in 1763
it is renowned to anglers the world over,
as manufacturers and suppliers of
fishing rods, flys and more recently
outdoor wear. Rods are still
manufactured here from imported cane
and many different flies are also made
for sale. Ashbourne was also the home
of Catherine Booth, the wife of General
Booth, the founder of the Salvation
Army. There is a plaque to her in
Sturston Road almost opposite the
garage, and a bust of her in the park.
The town is also famous for its
gingerbread and has a growing
reputation for its high class clothiers. A
recent feature of the town is Ashbourne
Water, which is pumped from the well at
the Nestlé factory. It is lightly
carbonated before being bottled and
marketed.

Although few of the villages in the

Village cross, Ilam

area have individual buildings of outstanding architectural merit, many are worth visiting. They are all villages which have enjoyed the patronage of some particular family. What does make them of interest is the variations of vernacular architecture, reflecting changing tastes and different building stones. Working northwards from Ashbourne, the most interesting villages are described briefly below.

Ilam village was rebuilt away from the hall in Tudor Gothic style in the early years of the nineteenth century. The hall was built for Mr Jesse Watts-Russell between 1821 and 1826, to the design of John Shaw, as a spectacular mansion with towers and turrets. This was during the era when Alton Towers was being

built in Tudor Gothic style under the influence of Pugin. The author considers that Ilam, built in the same style, was an attempt to 'keep up with the Jones's' — or in this case the Earl of Shrewsbury. Both properties were far too large for domestic comfort, but typical of Victorian affluence. The formal buildings of Ilam Hall were demolished in 1934 and the remaining portion is now a Youth Hostel, and not open to the public.

The 'model' village, school, hall and church at Ilam are all of interest. There is a National Trust Shop and Information Centre in the old cellar of the hall, while at the rear is a tea-room in the stable block of the Watts-Russell house. There are two Saxon crosses in

Fenny Bentley Old Hall

the churchyard and inside the church is the tomb of St Bertram and Francis Chantrey's statue of David Pike-Watts. The latter is very fine indeed and shows Jesse Watts-Russell's father-in-law on his death bed with his daughter and grandchildren at his bedside. The cross in the village near the bridge is dedicated to the daughter, Watts-Russell's wife, Mary. Also worth exploring are the paths in the wood in the grounds of the hall. One leads to a grotto where William Congreve wrote the *Old Batchelor,* and his stone desk and seat are still there. The path along the valley bottom, known as Paradise Walk, takes one past the resurging waters of the Manifold and Hamps. Further on it passes the 'Battle Cross' found when the village was remodelled. A visit to Ilam is a must for any holiday in the Peak.

Tissington is worth a visit too, particularly when the well dressing ceremony takes place. The hall is a large and very fine Jacobean mansion but not open to the public. It is a popular subject for photographers, along with the wells and village pond, while the old railway station site is an access point for the Tissington Trail.

Hartington is one of the major tourist centres of the Peak. The hall is dated 1611 and is now a Youth Hostel. The attractiveness of the village lies in the various houses around the square, which displays various forms of vernacular architecture. It is a sobering thought that this individuality of design and construction, all in houses built before planning constraints, seems to be so frowned upon by the planners today, although quite rightly they insist on buildings being built in the local stone. Hartington has several cafés, a good hotel, two gift shops and plenty of car parking. It is a good starting point for

Newhaven Hotel, a coaching inn on the Ashbourne-Buxton road

Hartington

Bunster Hill and Thorpe Cloud, Dovedale

Dove Holes, Dovedale

walks in the area — particularly into Dovedale.

Alstonfield to the south of Hartington is a fine village situated on the limestone plateau, with many solid buildings closely knit together. The church contains many seventeenth-century pews, a double-decker pulpit and a chest about ten feet long and probably 700 years old. Part of the building is Norman and a guide book is available in the church (and also at Hartington Church). In the village, there is a shop and café plus a good pub, The George Inn, well known to ramblers and tourists.

Walks in Dovedale and the Manifold Valley

In the dales, there are two places of particular interest which are worth visiting. The whole of the Dove between Hartington and the Stepping Stones near Thorpe is a well known beauty spot and if time does not permit a walk along the river, various roads give access by car. In the Manifold Valley the track-bed of the old railway has been surfaced with tarmac and now provides a useful footpath. A visit to Wettonmill, with its tea-room, and to Thor's Cave a mile or so downstream is essential. If you can find the time the whole track from Waterhouses to Hulme End is well worth walking, although it is a little hard underfoot, and return transport needs to be organised.

There is an abundance of delightful walks in the area. If you wish to walk the dales, there is of course Dovedale itself, between Ilam and Hartington. The dale is however being over-used and the tourist authorities no longer wax lyrical about its scenic qualities in order to encourage tourists to visit alternative areas. If you have not seen it, it must be said that it is not to be missed, but try incorporating part of it into a circular

walk, which has the advantage of allowing you to get away from the crowds.

Using Ilam as a base, a footpath at the foot of Bunster Hill via the Izaak Walton Hotel brings one to the river Dove which can be followed upstream to Ilam Rock. Cross the river here and head up Hall Dale to Stanshope. A path leads from here towards Wetton and upon reaching a narrow lane, the latter should be followed until a path enables you to head for Bincliffe Wood and eventually Castern Hall. This path overlooks the River Manifold and a nature reserve. At Castern, a road is reached which brings one back to Ilam. **9m**

From Hartington a path leads into the fields by the public toilets, heading for Beresford Dale. Upon reaching the road at Beresford Dale, where a footbridge and stepping stones cross the river, head for Alstonfield. Depending upon time, this can be either by continuing down Wolfscote Dale and turning uphill after crossing the Dove on a footbridge at Iron Tors, or a more direct route can be taken via Narrowdale. At Alstonfield, head directly to Wetton via Hope Marsh and upon arriving in Wetton take the path northwards between the twin humps of Wetton Hill returning to Hartington via Back of Ecton and Hulme End. If you don't like walking up the road from Hulme End to Hartington, you can head for Beresford Dale and return up river to your car. **5m** **5m**

The Manifold Valley has a tarmac surfaced path running down from Hulme End and then along the Hamps Valley from Beeston Tor to Waterhouses along the flat track-bed of the former Manifold Valley Light Railway. Circular routes involving the old railway line are numerous, but of course involve a climb up and out of the valley. Wettonmill is convenient and

Dovedale

Wettonmill Bridge, Manifold Valley

51

Lion Head Rock,
Dovedale

central point from which to start.

A short footpath from Wettonmill proceeding up the Hoo Brook towards Butterton brings one to a footbridge. The bridge is on a bridle road from Grindon to Waterhouses, which runs in almost a straight line between the two villages. A circular route can be made by proceeding south towards Grindon. In the last field before reaching the village another path can be taken which heads towards Ladyside Wood. Enter the wood over a stile by a stone trough and proceed through the wood slowly terracing around before dropping down into the Manifold Valley close to Thor's Cave. From the valley one can return to Wettonmill by following the former railway track up river. Alternatively cross the river at the footbridge and climb out of the valley heading towards Wetton and return to Wettonmill by the road. This latter alternative gives you superb views of both Thor's Cave and the valley.

At the footbridge on the Hoo Brook referred to above (GR 087555) you can turn northwards up the hill towards Warslow. After crossing the roads from Butterton to Wettonmill and Swainsley respectively, the path drops down to the Warslow Brook before climbing up to Warslow. Just before reaching the B5053 turn to the right and take the path which leads back to Swainsley. Here you can return down the valley to Wettonmill either on the old railway track which is flat, but often busy with

The village stocks, Warslow

traffic in the summer and at weekends, or alternatively by using the old road on the other side of the river. The latter is gated and therefore not used as much by traffic.

The whole eight miles of former railway track between Waterhouses and Hulme End is a useful path for the disabled both with or without wheelchairs or those with young children in pushchairs. Motor traffic is confined to a short section between Swainsley and Redhurst which is about half a mile below Wettonmill. Both Tissington Trail and the Cromford and High Peak Trail are also useful in this respect but the surface of the paths are not tarmaced like the Manifold track.

For a circular walk in the upper regions of the Dove and Manifold Valleys, park the car in Longnor and take the path from Folds End Farm down through the river meadows past Lower Boothlow Farm and on to Brund and then take the old packhorse route eastwards up the fields to Sheen. Cross the Sheen road by Lower House Farm and climb up hill to the ridge above Hartington where the path drops to a footbridge over the Dove before reaching Hartington by the side of the Stilton Cheese Factory. From the village take the gated road to Pilsbury and then the path past Pilsbury Castle and through the river meadows to Crowdecote, which leaves a short stiff climb back to Longnor.

There are numerous old packhorse routes in the upper reaches of both the Dove and Manifold. These are now preserved as footpaths and are all marked on the White Peak OS map. If you have both the time and inclination they offer a wonderful opportunity to explore this little known area.

3 South of the Wye

General Description

Much of the limestone district of the Peak lies south of Buxton, bounded to the west by the Dove and Manifold valleys and to the east by the river Derwent. East of Buxton, the river Wye dissects the limestone as it flows to join the Derwent. The district bounded by these valleys is a flattish plateau of interlocking stone walls forming a grey patchwork on a green quilt, and dissected by a number of picturesque dales. Occasionally, the relief is augmented by clumps of trees or sometimes long lines of trees growing along the old lead mine veins and providing shelter from the wind, which cuts almost through you in winter. Dotted over the landscape are countless farms, some in small clusters and less frequently, grouped together in villages. It is almost a pattern for the district to see the ribbon development of the last two and a half centuries now welded into neat little villages. A good example of the linear pattern can be seen at Youlgreave and is met again in Sheldon, Chelmorton, Taddington, Elton, Bonsall, Winster and Wensley amongst others.

This is an area where the motorist seems intent on passing through as he rushes between the tourist centres which surround it. It is however, worth while seeking out its treasures, whether it be the dales of the Lathkill and Bradford, buildings such as Youlgreave Church and Winster Market Hall or the archaeological remains such as Arbor Low stone circle and the smaller circles on Stanton Moor.

The underlying feature of most of the district is the limestone, although east of Youlgreave, both Harthill and Stanton moors consist of gritstone. Old quarries and lead mines abound and although the villages originally depended on a local well or spring for water, many of these have since dried up. Alteration in the water table from lead mining activities is often quoted as the cause, indeed, even some village ponds have suffered the same fate. In 1976, the river Bradford disappeared for several months, causing fears that the crystal clear waters had gone for good. Today, old lead mines drainage levels, or soughs (pronounced 'suffs') take a considerable amount of the surface water.

Historical Connections

Despite the presence of limestone, the number of caves is surprisingly small, Lathkill Head Cave being the only one of any size. Early man made use therefore, of the surface of the area for burial purposes and numerous tumuli can be found marked on the OS map. It is little wonder that Thomas Bateman lived in this district, at Middleton-by-Youlgreave, and there were few of these 'lows' as they are called which escaped his attention. The most fascinating, and of national importance, is Arbor Low, situated south of Monyash, and just off the Youlgreave to Parsley Hay road. This huge stone circle, now in the care of the Department of the Environment, consists of a ring of stones surrounded by a bank and ditch, the external diameter being nearly 300ft. It is now considered that the stones originally

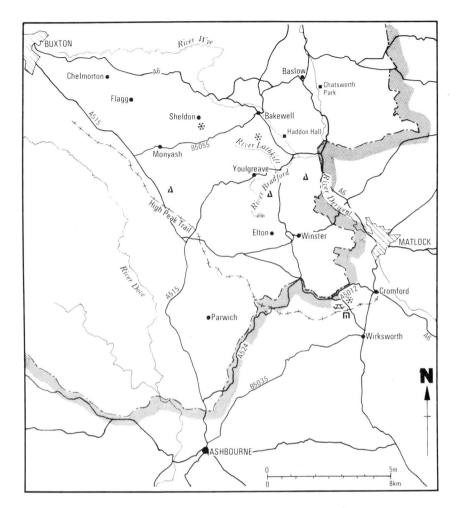

stood upright, although all but one have
fallen, and that there were originally
thirty-nine of them. Arbor Low has an
evocative atmosphere. Adjacent to it is
Gib Hill with an earlier henge. The
Roman road runs just to the west of Gib
Hill and an old trackway can be traced
between the two. It would seem that the
Roman surveyor made use of an already
existing prehistoric trackway.

Stanton Moor, to the east has an
impressive collection of five circles and
over seventy tumuli. The most
celebrated circle is the one known as the

Nine Ladies, which is not really a stone
circle but the remains of a large barrow
with the earth removed. The nine stones
still stand, albeit now surrounded by a
stone wall and with a further stone, the
King Stone, situated some 130ft away.
Many of these burial mounds and circles
have been excavated and an impressive
collection has been created by the late
Mr J.P. Heathcote and his father, which
may be seen at Sheffield Museum.

To the west, on Harthill Moor, lies
another circle — Nine Stones, although
only four stones now survive, together

Arbor Low

Although the Peak District has nothing comparable to Stonehenge, it does have many stone circles and Arbor Low is the best example. Its many stones lie fallen on the ground now, but it is not lacking in impressiveness because of this. The henge has a 'feel' about it. You can sense the unique setting appreciated by the Beaker people who built it. The views from here are impressive too. To the north, Sough Top dominates the horizon while to the west and east, stone-walled fields stretch to the tree-less gritstone moors.

Lathkill Dale

If you look over Lathkill Dale, about a mile or so out of Monyash on the Bakewell road, compare the fields either side of the dale. South of the river, the fields are noticeably larger. This is a relic of days when this area was enclosed in large fields by the monastic granges of Meadowplace and One Ash for sheep raising. Later enclosures generally produced smaller fields.

River Lathkill rises from a large cave entrance in wet weather, but parts of the river run underground in drought. The water in the trout pools is exceptionally clear.

Lathkill Dale lead mine once had one of the largest waterwheels in the country, being 52ft in diameter. Mandale lead mine has a ruined engine house, drainage sough, site of a huge waterwheel and remains of an aqueduct.

Magpie Lead Mine, Sheldon

Extensive surface remains of a major Peak District lead mine, including engine houses, chimneys, mainshaft and cage, etc. For access details contact Peak District Mining Museum at Matlock Bath.

Bradford Dale

Valley south of Youlgreave. Six crystal clear ponds, a packhorse bridge and a clapper bridge, add to the serenity of this delightful dale. The river Bradford flows from Middleton-via-Youlgreave to join the river Lathkill at Alport.

with the remains of an Iron Age fort, by Harthill Moor Farm. Nearby, a curious outcrop of rock is known as Robin Hood's Stride, or Mock Beggar's Hall. It has twin pinnacles, one at each end, and looks like the silhouette of a house. The rocks nearby contain a small cave, used as a shelter by a hermit in medieval times. The crucifix and a bench carved by its occupant still survives at the back of the shelter. Between Robin Hood's Stride and Hermit's Cave, is the ancient

trackway known as the Portway. This road was known to be an ancient trackway in Saxon times and from the nearby fort it descended to Alport where it can easily be followed over Haddon Fields as it makes for Ashford.

If you drive up the B5056 in a northwards direction along the Grangemill to Winster road, just to the north of Winster as one rounds a bend and reaches a bus stop, look to the skyline to the left of the road. This is a

An old milestone, Conkesbury Farm, Lathkill Dale.

good point to see Robin Hood's Stride, and also a track to a farm, which is the old Portway, and if you look carefully to the right of the track, the Hermit's Cave can be discerned.

The Anglo-Saxons have left us a remarkable artifact found in the Benty Grange tumulus, just north-west of Arbor Low. Here, Thomas Bateman uncovered the burial of a warrior and his helmet consisting of iron straps with a silver cross affixed to the nose-guard and surmounted by a bronze boar. A further remarkable find came from a barrow at Winster which yielded a cross of pure gold surmounted by a cut stone of garnet. It is richly carved and denotes the Christian influence which was beginning to penetrate the area. This and numerous other artifacts can be seen in Western Park Museum at Sheffield, which is well worth a trip on a wet day, particularly if you can combine it with a

visit to Abbeydale Industrial Hamlet on the A621 (just before its junction with the B6375). Many of the tumuli, including Benty Grange, were excavated by Thomas Bateman who lived at Lomberdale Hall near to Middleton-by-Youlgreave. It is still a private house and is not open to the public. Nearby in the village of Middleton is the Congregational Chapel which he had built and at the rear (also on private land but visible from the road) is his grave. Surrounded by iron railings, the grave is covered by a stone tomb, surmounted by a carved stone cinerary urn similar to those he unearthed.

Dales and Villages

The area covered by this chapter includes two of the most picturesque dales imaginable — Lathkill Dale and Bradford Dale. The clear waters in themselves are a striking attraction particularly when one has the time to watch the trout as they dart about. Lathkill Dale starts in an unpromising sort of way, half a mile to the east of Monyash. A footpath leaves the B5055 at the bottom of Bagshaw Dale and heads south westwards to Lathkill Dale. It is a convenient place to park one's car. Soon, small outcrops of limestone give way to a narrow, deep and steep sided valley, devoid of water and with a rocky floor. After about a mile, the river can usually be seen flowing from the mouth of a large cave on the right, known as Lathkill Head Cave. Despite its promising proportions it is in fact a very low cave inside for a considerable distance before solution cavities lead down to other levels. It is also dangerous in showery weather with only a limited period to get out if prolonged rain suddenly sets in. Further downstream at the foot of the dry valley leading up to Haddon Grove, lie the

Lomberdale Hall,
Middleton-by-Youlgreave

Bradford Dale

Lathkill Dale

ruins of Carter's Mill. This small cornmill was intact during the last war but is now reduced to ruins. Here, the valley becomes wooded and part of a Nature Reserve and the path follows the river amid leafy glades and old lead mining ruins. In summer, with the sun dancing on the pure water of the river, it is a delightful spot in which to spend one's time.

Soon after entering the wood a weir dams the river creating a small pool with the occasional duck swimming about. This pool provided a head of water for two waterwheels lower downstream and the water course or leat can be seen running horizontally down the valley. Further downstream there are several collapsed shafts of the Lathkilldale lead mine. The site of the old waterwheel pit can still be seen. Lower downstream, the leat crossed over the valley on an aqueduct with limestone piers which have been preserved in various stages of completeness. This brought the leat to the northern side of the river where it ran to Mandale lead mine. Part of the engine house remains here, together with its associated pumping shaft, which also had a waterwheel for pumping purposes. Obviously the expensive Cornish-type beam engine would only be used when water power was insufficient.

A few minute's walk from here is Lathkill Lodge where one may climb out of the valley to Over Haddon or southwards up the track and across the fields to Meadow Place Grange and Youlgreave. Unfortunately, the river bed is sometimes dry to this point which spoils the beauty of the spot. Downstream, a succession of eleven

weirs creates a marvellous sight but one needs to walk upriver to sustain the benefit of the view. At Conksbury, the old packhorse bridge carrying the Bakewell to Youlgreave road is crossed before continuing down the opposite bank towards Raper Lodge. Surprisingly unmentioned by Pevsner, this handsome house looks down on the river and another old packhorse bridge. Raper Lodge was featured in the film *The Virgin and the Gypsy* starring Franco Nero. Also featured was much of Youlgreave which is referred to as Congreave in the story, written by D.H. Lawrence. Lawrence was no stranger to the area, for he formerly stayed at Mountain Cottage, New Road, Middleton-by-Wirksworth.

The river meadows soon bring one to Alport with its seventeenth- and eighteenth-century cottages and ancient bridge, where the Lathkill meets the Bradford and closely hugs the road

before meeting the River Wye at Picory Corner.

The river Bradford commences south of Middleton, but the dale only becomes of consequence at Middleton where a track leads down to the dale. The track is a little rough underfoot and the bare limestone outcrops and overhanging trees give nothing away of the beauty of the dale beyond, as it brings one down to an old pumping station. The beauty of Bradford Dale lies in the six pools of crystal-clear water reflecting the mature trees, which line the sides of this steep sided dale at its upper end, downstream of this old pumping station. In the track between Middleton and the river the track side is a mass of yellow celandines in spring.

Youlgreave spills down into the dale, but the intrusion is a sympathetic one on the whole. A clapper bridge enables one to cross the river and either proceed downstream or walk up to the village.

Alport Bridge

Beyond the bridge, the path hugs the river until a road crosses the valley, which by now is getting much more shallow and open. Just beyond the road a bridge crosses the river yet again and a path follows the river down to Alport.

A further valley worth having a look at is the Via Gellia. Unfortunately it now has the A5012 running down it, and is much frequented by heavy lorries. It is named after the Gell family who own much land and still live at Hopton. They planted the trees in the dale, for which it is well known.

This part of the Peak now has two long distance paths which run along former railway lines; the Tissington Trail (formerly the Ashbourne-Buxton railway line) and the High Peak Trail which follows the old track bed of the Cromford and High Peak Railway (C &

HPR). The former railway was started in 1880 and closed partly in 1963, with the Hartington-Parsley Hay section closing in 1967. The trail runs from Ashbourne (just north of the tunnel) and skirts the villages of Thorpe, Tissington, Alsop-en-le-Dale and Hartington before terminating just south of Dowlow Quarry near to Buxton. The old stations are now car parks and picnic areas, with an information office in the former Hartington station signal box open to visitors during the summer weekends. In addition to stations near to these villages there are also car parks and picnic areas at Parsley Hay Wharf (where the Tissington Trail merges with the High Peak Trail) and at Hurdlow Wharf, on the Monyash to Longnor road.

The C & HPR was built to connect the Cromford Canal with the Peak Forest

17m

Canal and was built almost like a canal by a canal engineer. It was the only railway so built and it is not surprising to find long levels, steep inclines (in lieu of locks) and stations known as wharfs. Apart from Middleton Top engine house the signal box at Hartington, cuttings, embankments and inclines, there are few traces of the former railways, but the trails give easy access to a wide area of limestone countryside. The Peak Park Planning Board hires out cycles at Ashbourne and Parsley Hay and perhaps this is an ideal way of getting about. Certainly enough people use the scheme and venture away from the nearby villages, perhaps to do a circular route. The level nature of the trails, while ideal for cycles, can become less than exciting for the rambler, although the High Peak Trail does offer more of interest, while sections of both are suitable for the disabled. If you have not

ridden a bike for a while, you will find the High Peak Trail easier. It is flatter and surfaced with clinker rather than limestone. You will find it much easier to cycle north towards Parsley Hay on the Tissington Trail. If you are hiring your bike and making a circular trip, bear this in mind. Bikes may also be hired from Hartington.

The first section of the 33-mile long C & HPR (from Cromford to Whaley Bridge) was opened as early as 1830, and was one of the earliest lines in the country. Today the High Peak Trail stretches from Cromford Wharf on the Cromford Canal to just beyond Hurdlow Wharf. Access can be made to it at many places but perhaps the best are the old stations (or wharfs) at Hurdlow, Parsley Hay, Friden, Minninglow, Middleton Top engine house, Black Rocks and High Peak Juncion on the Cromford Canal. All of

18m

these places have a picnic area in addition to parking facilities.

3m   If you park at Minninglow (GR194582) and walk towards Friden, a walk of 1½ miles through the plantation the old railway brings one to a bend in the line near a farm. This is Gotham Curve, the tightest curve in its day on British Railways which turned the line through 80°! Further to the east at Hopton is one if the old inclines, originally worked by a stationary engine which hauled up the locos on a cable. This gradient was easier to tackle than the others on the line and the more modern and powerful locomotives could get up it unassisted. It was the steepest gradient worked on British Railways without assistance. It can easily be reached by taking the Wirksworth road from Brassington or alternatively the road to Hopton from the Via Gellia Valley. Middleton Top Engine, situated high above Middleton Village, still retains the beam engine that hauled the locos up the Middleton incline. It is usually open on Sundays and is in motion on the first Saturday in the month. It is a unique survivor of the very early railway era. It is easy to find because of its large chimney.

If a walk along the plateau stretch of the line is thought to be lacking in interest, then try the section from Black Rocks on the Cromford to Wirksworth road down to the Cromford Canal.   1¾m

Either arrange for someone to take a car around to the bottom, as there is a considerable drop in altitude, or walk a circular route to return to the car. A suggested route is to follow the canal to Whatstandwell. On route you pass the beam engine which pumped river water to the canal. It is preserved in a typical Victorian building and is open to the public. The huge engine, built in 1849, has now been restored to operating order. At Whatstandwell cross the river and take the path that runs westwards from a little north of Hankin Farm until the road is reached on Wirksworth Moor. This should be followed northwards to Bolehill and Black Rocks. This route gives one an opportunity of examining the buildings which survive at the High Peak Junction, together with

the catchpit near the bottom of Sheep Pasture Incline — complete with a railway wagon which ran away and was 'caught' in this safety device

In addition to the dales there are of course, the many villages which are scattered thoughout the area, chiefly in a linear pattern on the limestone platteau. They all have their own characteristics and space only permits a mention of some of them. In the north, Chelmorten lies besides a large hill, presumably on the site of a spring; it is an interesting place to examine. The oldest part of the village was obviously near to the hill and spring, which is why the church and pub now appear to be at the end of a cul-de-sac. With the coming of the first enclosure, land appears to have been alloted so that each cottage had a few

Derby Lane, Monyash, a typical 'green road'

Bunster Hill, Ilam

Ashbourne Church

Brassington

Monyash

Monyash

strips behind it and this order has been preserved, so that even today, there are many narrow fields stretching away; later enclosures resorted to a more regular pattern.

To the south-west lies Monyash. It was once an important centre of the lead mining industry, with a weekly market. Its old market cross still stands on the green, its base supposedly made from the old village stocks. The lead mining area of Derbyshire has its own Barmote Court — the oldest industrial court in the country, possibly a thousand years old. There were several courts now all held together at Wirksworth, but formerly Monyash and Winster had their own. The dependence of the area on agriculture is also expressed in the large village pond or mere. There were formerly four in the village but only this one remains. The pub is very popular with walkers and tourists, particularly in the summer as one can sit outside facing the village green.

Youlgreave is typical of the Peak District linear villages, with its sturdy church, displaying architecture spanning 800 years, standing in a dominating position at the end of the main street. It is an ideal spot from which to explore the Lathkill and Bradford Dales. It too was an important lead mining village and its many houses are old workers' cottages. Youlgreave Hall, standing close to the road, reminds one of Hartington Hall but lacks the granduer of the latter's setting, although they are comparable in age. The village is fortunate to have several shops,

The Market Hall, Winster

although the old Co-op is now a Youth Hostel. Look for the old circular stone water tank, or conduit head of 1849, built to provide a head of water when a public supply was first brought to the village. It is opposite the Youth Hostel.

To the south lies Winster, with a similar history of dependence on lead mining, demonstrated by the recent discovery of a water pressure engine in a nearby mine, now re-erected in the Peak District Mining Museum in Matlock Bath. It had originally been built at Coalbrookdale in 1819 for Alport mines,

near to Youlgreave, before being moved to Winster nearly thirty years later. Look for the Market Hall in the centre of the village, which was the first property acquired by the National Trust in Derbyshire. Pevsner describes it as being of the fifteenth or sixteenth century, but its original open ground floor arches have been built in with brick to give it more stability. It is open to the public and the National Trust maintains a small shop on the first floor. At the western end of the main street lies the hall which is early Georgian.

Winster Market Hall

In the middle ot Winster village stands the old market hall. It is now owned by the National Trust and the first floor has a small shop and information centre. It dates from the fifteenth or sixteenth century.

Rowter Rocks, Birchover

Once thought to have Druidical connections. Caves, rooms, steps, alcoves, armchairs, etc, carved from the rocks in the seventeenth century to form a retreat for the local vicar. The huge rocking stone no longer rocks.

Robin Hood's Stride (Mock Beggar's Hall) Birchover

Gritstone outcrop, most readily viewed from the A524 Winster to Haddon Road. Two 'chimneys' give the impression of a large building, especially at dusk. At the foot of the nearby Cratcliffe Tors is a medieval hermit's cave sheltered by an ancient yew tree. There is a crucifix carved on the wall and a niche for a lamp. The Portway, one of the Peaks oldest trackways passes nearby. To the north is Nine Stones Circle, with the tallest standing stones in the region, although only four survive. Castle Ring is a large Iron Age Hillfort, but it is difficult to appreciate its size as the path runs below the ramparts.

Stanton Moor

Open, heather-clad moors with some goods walks. Many archaeological sites including Nine Ladies Stone Circle. There are over seventy Bronze Age barrows on Stanton Moor and the artefacts are housed in Sheffield Museum. On the edge of the moor is a tower erected in 1832 as a tribute to Earl Grey for carrying the Reform Bill through Parliament.

Depending on time a drive around some of Winster's neighbouring villages should not be overlooked. There are some delightful corners to be seen in Stanton-in-the-Peak and Birchover, just to the north. The stone circles and Bronze Age tumuli on Stanton Moor have already been mentioned, but look out for the Cork Stone, Cat Stone and Andle Stone — huge natural blocks of gritstone, the latter havng footholes and iron handles for climbing to the top. The sharp-eyed visitor might find the rocks with dates and initials that were carved in the early nineteenth century by the Thornhill family of Stanton Hall. More obvious is the Earl Grey Tower, built in 1832 to celebrate the passing of the Reform Bill.

To the east on the minor road from Wensley to Matlock via Oaker hill, lies the tiny village of Snitterton with its lovely hall. There are many places of interest like these if one is prepared to go and seek out the backwaters.

Reference has already been made before in this chapter to the former lead mining activities. Old shafts abound in the area; indeed a current estimate is that as many as 100,000 shafts are scattered throughout the Peak. Many are of course shallow and blocked at the surface; others are deep; many are dangerous but only if not treated with

*Magpie Lead Mine,
Sheldon*

*Magpie Lead Mine,
Sheldon*

due respect. So much has been written on mining history that it would be pure repetition to include it here. Let us therefore be content to deal with only the theme of this book and concentrate on what there is for one to see and appreciate.

The region's lead mining museum will be dealt with under the Derwent Valley chapter but the area now under discussion contains some of the deepest and richest mines in the Peak. The most notable remains are those of Magpie Mine near to Sheldon. They can be seen from the Monyash to Ashford-in-the-Water road and details of access can be obtained from the Mining Museum. The remains have been preserved, including the remains of a Cornish type beam engine house, two chimneys, headgear, the winding drum of a steam whim and much else. A full description of the mine layout can also be bought from the museum. The remains in Lathkill Dale of Mandale Mine can also be visited.

Mining continues in the area for calcite is mined at Long Rake west of Youlgreave by a sister company of Friden works. Further opencast mining occurs north of Youlgreave for fluorspar. Also worthy of mention is the huge limestone mine at Middleton-by-Wirksworth being worked for a pure type of limestone used in the refining of sugar.

Just north of Middleton-by-Wirksworth lies Good Luck lead mine, which has been turned into a mine museum, and although it is still being explored and old passages dug out a lot of workings may be seen. It is open to the public but only if you are definitely prepared for it and are not claustrophobic. The passage is narrow in places, low in others, but gives a good impression of a typical lead mine of the area. Enquire at the Peak District Mining Museum in Matlock Bath for opening details.

To the south of the region lies Wirksworth. It would be easy to dismiss it as a drab town set amid the devastion of centuries of mining and quarrying. This would be unfortunate for there are several interesting buildings which are worth seeking out. The church is hidden behind the shops and several narrow passages — gennels in Derbyshire — give access to it. Even the main gates to the church are hemmed in between shops. The church contains a richly carved stone coffin lid of about AD 800, regarded as one of the most interesting Anglo-Saxon carvings in England.

If time does not permit a visit to the church, a path circles the churchyard creating a quiet backwater of peace and quiet. Walk around the north side of the church past the old Grammar School founded in 1576 and rebuilt in 1828 in a neo-Gothic style. Its battlements and pinnacles create a pleasing elevation worth looking at; it is now used for furniture manufacture. Continue past the old almshouses and turn north with the latter and the Grammar School on your left, to emerge into Coldwell Street. On your right is the old manse, a three-storey Georgian building standing opposite the older, early seventeenth-century Manor House, hidden behind its hedge.

Near the top of Coldwell Street towards the Market Place a passage on the right of the United Reform Church leads into Chapel Lane. On the left, some 200 yards or so up the lane stands the Moot Hall, referred to earlier, which was built in 1814. It still houses the oldest industrial court in the country and the standard measure for lead miners — a brass dish for measuring lead ore made in 1513. Return to Coldwell Street past the imposing Red

Wirksworth

The large church has a richly carved stone coffin lid of about AD800, found under the floor in 1820. Even though incomplete it depicts forty figures and is regarded as one of the most interesting early Anglo-Saxon remains in Britain. The churchyard is circular in shape — an indication of a very early Christian settlement.

Many historic buildings in the town have been refurbished and in 1983 Wirksworth was awarded the Europa Nostra Medal by the Council of Europe (the only one in Britain that year) for the improvements to the heritage of the town.

Wirksworth Moot Hall

The Moot Hall in Wirksworth houses the Barmote Court, the oldest industrial court in the country, thought to be a thousand years old. Here is housed the 14 pint lead dish, the standard measure for lead ore, which dates from 1513. The jurors still receive a clay pipe and tobacco to smoke in it after their meal!

Black Rocks Trail, Bolehill

Three woodland trails around the Black Rocks outcrop. Picnic area plus walk on the old Cromford and High Peak Trail. The gritstone rocks are popular with rock climbers.

Good Luck Mine, Via Gellia

If you would like to visit an old lead mine, enquire at the Peak District Mining Museum about the Good Luck Mine in the Via Gellia Valley, on the A5012 Cromford-Newhaven road (GR270566). It is usually open on the first Sunday in the month. It is narrow and has a low roof in places, but is typical of many small mines.

Middleton Top Winding Engine

The several inclines of the Cromford and High Peak Railway were overcome by erecting steam engines to haul or lower the locos and wagons which were attached to a cable worked by the steam engines. One of these survives at the top of Middleton Incline, west of Middleton-by-Wirksworth. The engine house is very conspicuous thanks to its tall chimney. Picnic site adjacent with a cycle hire centre.

Lion pub and cross the main road. Have a look at Symonds House (Number 15) across the road from the Red Lion, together with the recently restored seventeenth-century former house behind it in Dale End. Climb up the lane until one reaches Babington House on the left. It is a stiff climb up Greenhill to it but the house is worth seeing. Pevsner attributes it to the early seventeenth century, although on a modern porch is the date 1588.

Walks in the Area

This area contains some of the most attractive scenery in the Peak District and therefore the chance to spend a few memorable hours out walking should not be missed. A marvellous circular walk can be made involving both Lathkill Dale and its tributary the river Bradford. Park your car at the picnic

6½

Clapper bridge, Bradford Dale

area on Long Rake due west of Youlgreave (GR 194645). Take the road towards Conksbury and upon reaching the third field on the left take the path to Meadow Place Grange. Proceed through the farmyard and cross the field to reach

Old toll house, Wensley

Meadow Place Wood where a track leads down to Lathkill Lodge and the river Lathkill. Take the path downstream to Conksbury Bridge and ensure that you look back at least once or twice, to catch the memorable sight of the water flowing over the many weirs a quarter of a mile above the bridge. Cross the bridge and almost opposite Conksbury Farm take the path which leads past Raper Lodge to Alport. Cross over the road to Youlgreave and take the path up the river Bradford. Below Youlgreave the first of six delightful pools of crystal clear water is reached. After passing the sixth climb out of the valley to Middleton and then take the path at the side of the road to Lomberdale Hall. At GR 641199 take the path which crosses the road to

Friden and climb up through the fields back to the picnic site.

The rest of Lathkill Dale should not be missed and the path should be taken upstream from Lathkill Lodge towards Monyash. The first half of the valley is wooded and by and large this is also the most interesting part of the valley. The source of the river Lathkill is passed at Lathkill Head Cave before reaching Monyash. Return via the path from Manor House Farm which crosses Ferndale before reaching One Ash Grange Farm. From here proceed to the picnic area on Long Rake via Callinglow Farm and then return to Lathkill Lodge via Meadow Place Grange as described above. It should be noted that cars should be parked at the car park in Over Haddon and not at Lathkill Lodge.

4 The Northern Limestone Plateau

The river Wye rises on Axe Edge and flows down to Buxton before turning eastwards to divide the limestone region into two. Its deeply cut valley does this quite effectively and today much of its course north of Rowsley is followed by the A6 trunk road. The valley has two quite distinct features. North-west of Bakewell it is narrow and deeply incised with sheer limestone bluffs which even overhang the river in places. It is joined by many tributary valleys, mostly quite deep but chiefly devoid of water: Great Rocks Dale, the two Deep Dales, Monks Dale, Tideswell Dale, Cressbrook Dale and Taddington Dale being the largest. South-east of Bakewell, the river flows across softer, later rocks which have eroded more easily creating a wider valley.

Fortunatley, the A6 road took advantage of Taddington Dale and so spared perhaps the most beautiful part of the Wye, between Topley Pike and the bottom of Monsal Dale. Part of this can be viewed from the car, but much is preserved for the rambler, including the most interesting parts of Chee Dale, Water-cum-Jolly Dale and parts of Monsal Dale.

North of the Wye, the limestone plateau is dissected by the tributary valleys mentioned above. It stretches as far north as Castleton and Eyam and includes some minor hills such as Longstone Edge, Bradwell Moor and Eldon Hill. It is an area of dry stone walls and dry valleys with dairy and

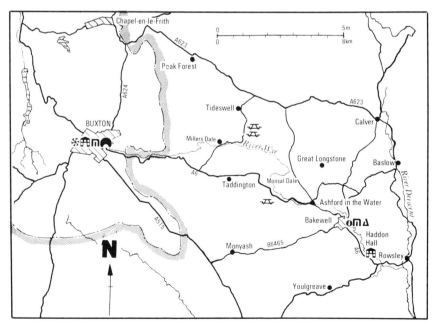

sheep farms. It has been an important area for quarrying and lead mining too.

Early History of the Area

The area was also of importance to man in early times. When the Romans arrived they found a small, but presumably effective, system of Iron Age forts and routes connecting them. The ancient Portway which came north from Derby crossed through the area. From Wirksworth, the road headed via Grangemill for the Iron Age fort north west of Winster above Robin Hood's Stride. From there, it made for Alport and crossed the high ground west of Bakewell before descending to the village of Ashford where it forded the Wye. It is easy to see the Portway at Ashford descending down to the river. Ashford was an important crossing place of the River Wye and the ancient Portway was used for centuries as a major highway. Indeed, north of the village, it is now tarmac-covered and is still in use as part of the road to Wardlow and Foolow.

The importance of Ashford is reflected in the establishment of a castle north of the church although nothing remains except for a few place names, including Castlegate, the current name for the Portway north of the village. From Ashford, the Portway proceeded to Monsal Head along the existing roadway and then on to Wardlow Mires where it probably branched, heading through the fields to an Iron Age camp at Burr Tor, close to the gliding club, and then on to Bradwell via Robin Hood's Seat. The alternative route from Wardlow Mires took a more direct route to Bradwell via Windmill. Somewhere along the road between Ashford and Monsal Head, a track would have branched off to the west to the Iron Age fort at the top of the promontory known

as Fin Cop. There is no public right of way to the fort but the site can perhaps best be appreciated from the west of the River Wye. Fin Cop is visible for a considerable distance and with its two very steep sides almost 90° to each other it would have presented a visually impressive and physically an important defensive position. It is perhaps best photographed fron the west also, a good vantage point being from Taddington village.

Of great antiquity even in Iron Age times were the tumuli and stone circles. Just to the north of Tideswell is Tideslow, the largest tumulus in the Peak District. Perhaps of more interest is Five Wells just north of the farm of that name which is situated on the path between Chelmorton and Taddington, as it crosses Sough Top. In fact it can also be seen from the A6 near the Waterloo public house, standing out on the skyline. Five Wells is a chambered burial which was uncovered during excavation. It is apparently the highest situated cairn in the country at 1,400ft, and relics from here and other prehistoric sites can be seen in Buxton Museum.

Buxton, Bakewell and the Wye Valley

Buxton itself has an ancient history. It attracted the Romans because of its warm mineral water which bubbles up to the surface. They built a bath here and called their settlement *Aquae Arnemetiae.* To the bath came Roman roads from Derby, Leek, Brough (*Navio*) east of Castleton, and south from near Glossop from a fort probably called *Ardotalia* but more popularly known by the fictitious *Melandra*. Other roads came from the west and the north-west. A Roman milestone found in 1856 is now preserved in the museum.

After the Romans left, the spring was

not entirely forgotten and by Tudor times it had a reputation for curing invalids. Mary, Queen of Scots, while a prisoner in the custody of William, Earl of Shrewsbury, came here to seek relief from rheumatism. The Crescent, built adjacent to the spring, was designed by John Carr of York the fifth Duke of Devonshire. It was built between 1780 and 1790 and was the first important imitation of the Royal Crescent at Bath, as part of a deliberate plan by the Duke to build Buxton into a Spa town to rival Bath. Its cost, according to Pevsner, was £38,000 which means it could have been financed out of a single year's profit from the Ecton Mine in the Manifold Valley, as is traditionally held. It was built primarily as a hotel and shopping complex and was partly occupied from

---

PLACES OF INTEREST IN AND NEAR BUXTON

Buxton was famous in olden times for its spa water and this still bubbles to the surface. The Opera House has recently been restored and details of its full programme are readily available in the area.

The Crescent
Built by the Duke of Devonshire in the 1780's and the first important imitation of the Royal Crescent at Bath. The ceiling in the assembly room (now the Public Library) is particulary impressive.

Buxton Micrarium, The Crescent
An exhibtion of nature beneath the microscope. Situated opposite The Crescent in the former Pump Room. It is the world's first 'planetarium' of the microscope, allowing visitors to explore for themselves the fascinating world under the microscope.

Buxton Museum and Art Gallery,
Terrace Road
Collection of archaeological remains found in local caves, a Roman milestone, etc. Small geological collection including exquisite specimens of Blue John stone from Castleton.

Solomon's Temple
Situated on Grinlow is a small folly which can be seen from many directions. Considerable panoramic view from the temple.

Pooles Cavern, Green Lane
After a period of closure this show cave, in the southern suburbs of Buxton, has been reopened. In addition to the cave, there is a country park extending to 100 acres with a picnic area and free car park. There is also an exhibition room with an audio-visual aid.

Peak Forest Canal
Canal basin at Bugsworth (now Buxworth) near Whaley Bridge with old warehouses etc. Imposing set of stair locks at Marple Bridge and large aqueduct over the river Goyt, some 80ft high.

The Wye Valley

The river Wye flows through a series of dales which should not be missed. The first dale out of Buxton has been spoilt by the A6 and a sewerage works, particularly, but beyond Topley Pike the scenery is more peaceful. The river flows through Chee Dale, Miller's Dale, Water-cum-Jolly Dale to reach Monsal Dale which can be followed on foot down to the A6 at the foot of Taddington Dale (and even further towards Bakewell if you wish). Do not overlook the tributary dales of Monks Dale, Tideswell Dale and Cressbrook Dale.

Monsal Dale

Panoramic viewpoint with views down to the river Wye at Monsal Dale and including the well known, handsome railway viaduct of the Buxton to Bakewell line, much criticised by John Ruskin when it was originally built in the 1860s.

Monsal Trail

Recently opened footpath on former railway line down the Wye Valley. The tunnels are closed and an alpine-type path may be used over the tunnels. Spectacular views in places. Not recommended for cyclists or if you are not sure-footed.

Cressbrook Mill, Monsal Dale

Attractive Georgian-style four-storey former textile mill dating from 1815. The large millpond occupied what is now known as Water-cum-Jolly-Dale, where the river has been dammed to provide a head of water for the mill. The dale is as delightful as its name and is worth going to see if your itinerary does not include a walk down this particular section of the river Wye.

Tideswell

An interesting village to explore including its historic church known as 'The Cathedral of the Peak'. There are shops, banks, restaurants and other more urban facilities available here.

Wormhill

Memorial to James Brindley, the canal engineer, who was born in the village. If you drive to Wormhill from Tideswell, look for the hall and the carved fifteenth-century cross as you pass through the hamlet of Wheston.

1786. At the north end was the Great Hotel, now the library. The library is worth a visit particularly to the Assembly Room upstairs to view its ceiling, now carefully restored and decorated by Derbyshire County Council.

Patronage by the Devonshire family continued with the building of the stables to the rear of The Crescent during 1785-90. This was converted to the Devonshire Royal Hospital in 1859, and the central courtyard for exercising the horses was covered with a dome in 1881-2. At the time, it was the largest dome in the world being 156ft in diameter and it weighs 560 tons!

Adjoining The Crescent are the

thermal and natural baths; the latter at the south end and the former at the northern end, but both appear to be little used now. Behind The Crescent is the Pavilion, Opera House and Pavilion Gardens. The Gardens are worth a visit, as is also the recently restored and re-opened Opera House,which has already gained a high reputation for the quality of its performances.

There is much else to see in Buxton. A walk down Spring Gardens, the main shopping street, is recommended. The town, the highest in England, has a railway station, good bus services and municipal conveniences such as the Pavilion Gardens, bowling greens and two golf clubs. It also has a Youth Hostel at Sherbrook Lodge, set amid the trees opposite the hospital.

South of the hostel and the town, on Grin Low, is Solomon's Temple. This folly was built to provide labour for out-of-work men. It is worth visiting if only for the panoramic view over Buxton. Northwards lie the high moorland of Combs Moss and Shining Tor; to the south-west is Axe Edge, and south-eastwards can be seen Sough Top and the green fields and grey walls of the White Peak. The neat fields and clumps of trees of the limestone area contrasts vividly with the rugged treeless moors of the western edge of the Peak.

The northern portion of the limestone region has many similarities to the area south of the Wye valley. A rolling landscape of green fields with an intricate system of dry stone walls is synonymous with the Peak District limestone region as a whole. Other than the River Wye itself however, the area is devoid of any river system. It is of course bounded in the east by the River Derwent, but this flows through the gritstones of the eastern edge.

There are no counterparts for the river systems of the Dove, Manifold, Lathkill

River Wye at Shacklow

and its smaller tributary, the Bradford. The presence of several dry valleys has already been indicated and while pleasant enough, they lack the attractions that flowing water can create. The most interesting dale therefore is that of the Wye. It is crossed by a road at Miller's Dale, there is a minor road to Litton, and a road to Cressbrook and Wardlow Mires drops into the dale at Monsal Head. A little further south, the A6 runs up the valley to the bottom of Taddington Dale and returns to it for the section between Topley Pike and Buxton. There is much to see on foot and fortunately the linear pattern of the valley can be overcome by catching a bus back to one's starting point if need arises. Buses run between Buxton and both Tideswell (for Sheffield) and Bakewell (for Derby and Chesterfield).

Topley Pike (GR 103725) offers a good place to start. One can park opposite Tarmac's Quarry at this point, where a minor road turns down to the river. It is marked on the OS 'The White Peak' Map. This track follows the river down to the bottom of Great Rocks Dale, which houses ICI's quarry, with the longest quarry face in Europe. The track passes through well wooded surroundings, sharing the narrow valley with the railway which crosses three times overhead. Upon reaching the footbridge and the row of cottages — presumably built for workers of the disused quarry behind — one also leaves Wye Dale for Chee Dale. Below here, the dale becomes much more interesting and in bad weather, even adventuresome!

For most of the way, the path hugs the river, but in places it becomes precipitous particularly where it runs on the south side of the river near to the railway arch, and also just upstream from Flag Dale. The valley is characterised in places by sheer limestone bluffs, several of which overhang the valley bottom. In two places, this forces the path into the river and onto stepping stones. If the river is in flood, the dale can be quite impassable. The outcrop of limestone, some with sheer waterworn slabs and overhangs offer considerable sport to climbers. The valley is well wooded in places which offers some variety of scenery. It would be easy to overstate the

Great Rocks Dale

scenery of the dale, but if you sometimes get bored with the almost regularity of the beauty and river-side paths in some of the other dales, remember Chee Dale.

A little beyond Flag Dale, the valley opens out a little as one approaches the footbridge carrying the path from Wormhill to Blackwell over the river. Beyond here it is just a short walk into Miller's Dale. In former days Miller's Dale was an important place locally. It not only served as a railway station for many surrounding villages, including Tideswell, but Manchester to Derby through trains stopped here to pick up passengers from Buxton. The passenger traffic, together with the limestone traffic, made Miller's Dale a big station for its location. The Tideswell-Taddington road crosses the valley here too and river, road and railway are neighbours yet again. There are in fact, two quite impressive railway bridges

situated side by side, the initial bridge being augmented in 1903 by the second one, forty years after the line opened. Commerce also dictated a road down the dale at this point to serve Litton Mill. Originally it was a waterwheel driven textile mill, and it still operates although the original importance of the site has been superseded. The mill earned a reputation for the unfortunate excesses of child labour in the early nineteenth century, epitomised in Walter Unsworth's novel *The Devil's Mill*. The path down the dale proceeds through the millyard, where the road ends.

Beyond here lies Water-cum-Jolly Dale. One wonders whether the impounded water, backing up from Cressbrook Mill inspired the name or whether it dates from a time prior to this. On a summer's day the broad expanse of water with the waterworn limestone bluff behind reflecting in the

79

millpool and the occasional duck or
moorhen on the surface adds to the
tranquillity of the dale.

Cressbrook Mill no longer operates.
The main four-storey structure which
dates from 1815 replaced an earlier mill
built by Arkwright in 1779. Of interest is
his apprentice house by the mill race,
looking like a Gothic castle, with narrow
lancet windows and turrets. Today this
elegant mill crowned by a cupola looks
forlorn but it is slowly being restored.

Monsal Dale

The Old House Museum,
Cunningham Place, Bakewell
A restored sixteenth-century house,
situated behind the church, with
original wattle and daub interior
walls. Industrial archaeology
collection including early Arkwright
machinery.

The Market Hall, Bakewell
The Information Centre in the centre
of Bakewell is situated in the old
market hall. The centre features a
display of different aspects of the
Peak District National Park and
there are a variety of publications
issued by the National Park on sale.

Bakewell Church
Fourteenth century with a
considerable collection of early
medieval monuments, including that
to Dorothy Vernon and Sir John
Manners, who are said to have
eloped from Haddon Hall. There are
many fragments of Saxon carvings in
the porch and two Saxon cross shafts
in the churchyard.

Holme Bank Chert Mine
Just to the north of Bakewell is an
old chert mine. Blocks of chert used
to be sent to the Potteries where they
were used in the grinding of calcined
flint for bone china. The mine is now
being developed as a tourist
attraction and this includes a trip into
the old galleries.

Haddon Hall, Near Bakewell
Situated on the A6 south of the town.
A magnificent medieval house,
regarded as the finest of its kind in
Britain, little altered since the
sixteenth century, with much fine oak
panelling, furniture and gardens.

Hassop Hall
North of Bakewell lies Hassop with
its imposing hall, the home of the
Eyre family, who also built the
classical style church in the village.
Hassop Hall is a magnificent
building. Although not as big as
Thornbridge Hall a few miles away at
Great Longstone, the house is
augmented by some fine buildings at
the rear plus its gate house and dower
cottages. It is also now a hotel and
restaurant and therefore parts may be
inspected after your meal.

On the south side of the mill, more
recent additions add little of aesthetic
value. Downstream from the mill the
path follows the lane to Monsal Head.
Do not take the first bridge across the
river, but take the second, situated
where the road begins to rise towards
Monsal Head. The path goes through
the arches which carried the railway line
to Buxton from Bakewell. Ruskin
strongly objected to the intrusion of the
railway, but the line has mellowed into
the landscape and the view point from
Monsal Head is now, ironically, well
known and popular with photographers.
Just downstream from the railway
arches the River Wye tumbles over a
weir which many of people must
recognise from the numerous postcards
and calenders in which it features. From

here the path cuts through the meadows at the bottom of the wood to meet the A6 at the foot of Taddington Dale where there is a picnic site, car park and toilets.

Below Taddington Dale, the river meanders slowly to Ashford-in-the-Water and Bakewell. A footpath follows much of the route, passing through Great Shacklow Wood, emerging by the river close to where the water flowing down Magpie Sough reaches the Wye. The sough (pronounced 'suff') drains Magpie Mine, situated over a mile away south of Sheldon village. The entrance or sough-trail is new and gated, the old entrance having been re-opened recently after being in a collapsed state for several years. The path is an easy walk amid a leafy glade, reaching the fields by an old watermill, now being restored. There are three waterwheels here; two are attached to the mill buildings and there is a third and much smaller one which was used to pump water up to Sheldon village before mains water was laid.

After a short walk through the fields the path reaches Kirkdale and the road to Sheldon. The works depot here used to be a marble mill and many of the black marble slabs visible in Derbyshire churches were cut and polished here. The stone, which is really a dark limestone which takes a high polish and looks like marble, was mined from two localities nearby. Not far away was found a rare red coloured deposit of limestone and occasionally examples can be found in local churches. The marble works lost some of its buildings when the Ashford bypass was built, which spared the village much heavy traffic, Ashford is worth a look around, particularly to view the old packhorse bridge — Sheepwash Bridge — and its neighbouring pump shelter, although the village pump has now gone. The village was once of at least equal importance to Bakewell, but that has all changed now. As early as the

Ashford in the Water

Sheepwash Bridge, Ashford in the Water

seventeenth century, 300 packhorses, laden with malt, passed northwards through the village each week.

Parts of the former railway track between Buxton and Rowsley have been developed into the Monsal Trail. The trail commences in the north at Blackwell Mill Cottages at the top of Chee Dale and at the south, at Coombs Road Viaduct south of Bakewell. At Blackwell Mill Cottages, instead of crossing the river, a footpath leads uphill to the old railway. Follow the railway line and after about one mile, a tunnel is reached which is currently unsafe and a descent must be made to the river. At the time of writing it is probably best to regain the trail at Millers Dale station. A further two tunnels exist below Litton Mill which must also be by-passed.

There is a plate layer's path which may be used with care, or alternatively, cross the river at Litton Mill over the footbridge, and follow the river down to Upperdale. Here a road crosses the river and the railway may be rejoined near Putwell Mine, indentifiable by its small chimney.

If you use the plate layer's path, the views into the dale are superb. However it is not recommended if you are not sure-footed or if you are nervous of heights. Also, it is essential to keep an eye on young children. Nonetheless, it is worth walking and we are fortunate that the Planning Board had the foresight to open it up.

Upon crossing the famous viaduct over the River Wye, it is necessary to leave the line because of another tunnel.

The Market House, Bakewell

Climb out of the valley up the steps to Monsal Head. From here, take the road to Little Longstone, where a path leads back to Ashford and gives access to the line again. There are no problems for the rest of the way to Bakewell. This is a useful trail despite the obvious problems of the tunnels and it enables one or two circular routes to be planned which were not possible before. Currently, the track is still surfaced with railway ballast. Although the other trails in the Peak may be used by the disabled, cyclists or horses, this trail is not recommended at the present time for these uses.

Bakewell is the central town of the Peak and attracts many thousands of visitors. It has some interesting groups of buildings and a good selection of shops, both for provisions and souvenirs. Its bookshop carries a wide range of books and papers on the Peak District. Several shops offer Bakewell puddings, preserving the memory of the

culinary accident that produced the new dish. The disaster apparently occurred at the Rutland Arms when the cook put the jam at the botton of the dish instead of on top of the pastry as is usual.

Although much of Bakewell is comparatively recent, as much building took place from late Victorian times onwards, the town centre does have some fine buildings which are worth looking at and some are quite old. The National Park Information Office is situated in the former Market Hall which dates from the early seventeenth century. Rutland Square — where the roundabout now is — was set out in 1804 when the Rutland Arms was built. This is a fine coaching inn and its stable still remains across the road, the buildings being built around two courtyards, one behind the other.

The Bath Gardens adjacent to the Old Rutland Hotel stables used to be the gardens to Bath House built by the

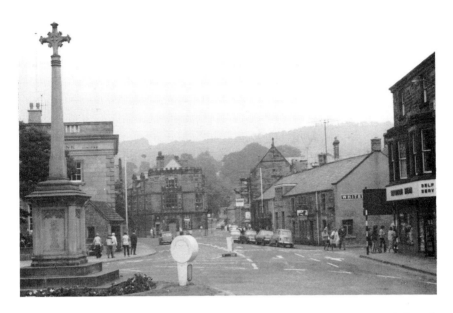

Rutland Square, Bakewell

Duke of Rutland in 1697 over a natural spring. Bath House is the last building on the left at the Bath Street end of the gardens and is now occupied by the British Legion. The duke's bath still survives in the cellar and is 33ft by 16ft in extent! Bakewell failed, however to develop as a spa town like Buxton and Matlock.

Behind the hotel is a small area of old houses which reward investigation. Just up the road to Monyash is the old town hall on the right, one of the most interesting buildings in the town. Behind is the church, situated on an elevated site with its steeple dominating the skyline. There are two ancient crosses in the churchyard, of the ninth and eleventh centuries. The one beneath the eastern end of the church was found in Two Dales, north of Matlock.

The church itself dates from Norman times. Much of the structure had been built by the end of the fourteenth

century and Pevsner regards the accumulatd headstones and coffin slabs, housed in the south porch, as the largest and most varied group of medieval monuments housed in the United Kingdom. They were found during restoration work in 1841-2. Some of the stones date from the Anglo-Saxon period and these presumably include the scroll work in pieces to the right as one goes through the porch. More of these carved stones can be seen on the west wall of the nave. Bakewell Church is worth a look around, but it is perhaps not so interesting to the casual visitor as Tideswell. Also, on my visit, there was no leaflet describing the church and its architecture as there is at Tideswell.

To the west of the church is the Old House Museum. It was built in 1543 and has been restored by the Bakewell Historical Society. Just to the north of the church is Bagshaw Hill, and halfway down is Bagshaw Hall, built in 1684. To

Bakewell Bridge

the rear is Bakewell Youth Hostel, built in the Hall's former kitchen garden. To complete a circular tour of the town centre, cross the A6 at the bottom of Bagshaw Hill and walk past the Millford Hotel to the mill leat of Victoria Cornmill (which still has its iron waterwheel in the millyard, having been lifted out of the wheelpit for restoration). Turn downstream and follow the leat to Castle Street which brings you out by the bridge over the River Wye which was

Holme Bridge, Bakewell

built in 1300. Just a little upstream is Holme Bridge, a packhorse bridge built in 1694 and now a footbridge.

Perhaps the main point of interest of Bakewell is that it acts as a centre for visiting different parts of the Peak and of course the two major houses of the area — Chatsworth and Haddon Hall. The latter lies just down the river from the town and is a must for any visitor. It is very much older than Chatsworth, and is claimed by many to be the country's most complete fortified house.

Haddon Hall stands adjacent to the A6, hidden by trees and a beech hedge. The car park is across the road, so that one approaches the gatehouse on foot. The entrance is impressive with two lines of mature beech hedges converging at an old packhorse bridge over the shallow waters of the River Wye. The house itself stands on a bluff overlooking the river and the bridge, although somewhat masked by the trees and the entrance is at the foot of the north-west tower with a very low doorway.

The battlemented buildings are set around two courtyards paved with flagstones. In the south-west corner of the hall and lower courtyard is situated the chapel. This is probably the oldest part of the hall for parts of the chapel were built by William Peveril around 1080-1090. The alter slab in the south aisle of the chapel is of Norman origin as are the two fonts in other parts of the chapel. It has a three decker pulpit and various pews built by Sir George Manners in 1624. The chapel is very well lit by natural means and remarkably well preserved. It contrasts greatly with the chapel of Chatsworth which is

Haddon Hall, the banqueting hall

Haddon Hall, the lower courtyard

resplendent in all its richness.

The old kitchens are on the left of the entrance hall and still retain such items as bowls carved in the wooden bench tops. Beyond the kitchen is the bakehouse and butcher's shop which provided essential food for the house. The entrance hall opens into the banqueting hall which was built around 1350 by Sir Richard Vernon, and this is essentially as he built it with oak panelling and a minstrel's gallery. The long table in the hall is 400 years old and contrasts with the roof above it, which had to be replaced in 1924. Even so the new roof is a genuine attempt to recreate the style of the old. Off the banqueting hall is the dining room which dates from 1500 and was added by Sir Henry Vernon. This is a delightful room with much carved panelling showing the coat-of-arms of the Talbot family and Edward VI when Prince of Wales. Above the dining room on the first floor

is the great chamber with a remarkable number of tapestries plus moulded plaster work. In a succession of rooms the visitor's notes advise of architectural details dating parts of the building to around 1500 or even earlier. Haddon Hall is an amazing survival, in a very good state of repair, of this period of English architecture. The long gallery with its heraldic glass window dates from 1589, beautifully carved stone mullions, and panelled walls carved as long ago as the middle of the sixteenth century make this one of the most beautiful rooms in the house.

Haddon Hall is of course famous for the love story concerning Dorothy Vernon, the wife of John Vernon. Her elopement in 1563 with John Manners was imortalised by Sir Walter Scott, and just off the long gallery one can still see the steps down which she is supposd to have eloped with her lover. In the latter half of the seventeenth century the Duke

The Peacock Hotel, Rowsley

Old toll house, Little Rowsley

of Rutland moved his family seat to Belvoir Castle in Leicestershire, so that during the next 200 years the hall became more or less empty and unused, although still maintained. This is the reason why the hall was never 'restored' or rebuilt. Today it represents a microcosm of life in a country house over four hundred years ago.

Just below Haddon lies Rowsley. Here, the Lathkill joins the Wye at Picory Corner and the combined waters flow towards the Derwent. Rowsley is a small village: the surprising thing about the place is that it not much larger. It

used to boast a substanial railway marshalling yard — a relic of the days when Rowlsey was the rail head of the Midland Railway's line from Derby and prior to the building of the connection with Buxton which began in 1860. It boasts a very fine hotel, the Peacock, originally built in 1652 and later became a dower house of Haddon Hall. Of particular interest to residents and visitors alike is a ceramic peacock just inside the entrance. It is one of five made by Minton of Stoke-on-Trent in 1850-1, and this one went down with the ship *Loch Ard* in 1878, fourteen miles off

Moonlight Heads, Victoria, Australia. It was brought up during salvage operations, and eventually came back to England. Minton's have apparently traced four of their peacocks and a lady visitor from Australia told the hotel that she had number five, also brought up from the hapless *Loch Ard*. At Rowsley the River Wye joins the Derwent, flowing south from the northern gritstone moors past Calver and Chatsworth.

North of the Wye

The limestone region north of the River Wye is an interesting one. It is a patchwork of small villages and undulating farmland cut by some rather deep valleys, such as Cressbrook Dale, Coombs Dale and Middleton Dale. To the east it is overlooked by Longstone Edge, with the scar of High Rake Mine. The latter was once the scene of the worst financial lead mining venture in the whole of the Peak and is now an opencast site, worked more recently for fluorspar rather than lead ore.

Leaving out Eyam, which is situated on the edge of the gritstone and is reserved for a later chapter, the largest village is Tideswell. There must be many visitors to the Peak who miss — or drive straight through — Tideswell. With its multitude of shops — including a Co-op, a chemist, two restaurants, banks and petrol station — it can offer most things a visitor needs. It is a medley of small buildings in rows and little nooks. It has even a gas supply, to the envy of many other Peakland villages.

The area around the church is a pure gem, even though at first glance it does not give the impression of being anything special. Park near the church, and have a look at the George Hotel, a fine coaching inn with Venetian windows and dating from 1730. To the rear of the church is the vicarage and at its side a superb example of vernacular architecture, combining cut blocks of limestone with gritstone quoins and mullions.

The entrance to the church is also on the far side. Fortunately for visitors, a

Tideswell

Litton

Village Well, Foolow

91

leaflet gives a concise history of the building for there is much to see in the church. There is a wealth of different brasses, some very old, including one showing Bishop Pursglove of Hull and a native of Tideswell, in full eucharistic vestments as worn before the Reformation. The original building was enlarged in the fourteenth century and is very impressive; it is certainly a must for the discerning visitor and fully lives up to its title of 'Cathedral of the Peak'.

Elsewhere, the villages follow the familiar pattern, either elongated or set around a village square. Most are very small but with little features here and there that make a visit worthwhile — the stocks in Litton; the fourteenth-century cross and adjacent village pond in Foolow; the memorial to James Brindley at Wormhill where he was born, all spring to mind. East of Litton, on the road to Wardlow Mires is the top of Cressbrook Dale, its steep sided valley coming right up to the road. A pronounced feature of this end of the valley is Peter's Stone which is a detached block of limestone of significant size. It can be viewed from the A623 at Wardlow Mires also, but the signposted footpath from there down the top of the dale enables you to get quite close. It is also the outcrop depicted with a wheatear on the front of the White Peak OS Map.

Mention of the fourteenth-century

Peter's Stone,
Cressbrook Dale

Foolow

cross in Foolow has been made above. It is worth more than a passing glance; indeed much can be missed by not stopping and having a look around. The cross was erected on the green in 1868 at the rear of a flat stone with an iron ring set in its top surface. The stone is a bullbaiting stone and must be very old, for bull baiting was made illegal in 1835. The cross stands by the old village mere, fed by a spring with a wall around it. Around this centre sit the village school, manor house, pub, and chapel and other old village buildings dating from the seventeenth and eighteenth centuries. Although Foolow looks a small village of little interest, this is not the case, as perhaps the above indicates. This is not confined to this one village for there is much to be found in most of our Peakland villages, if you care to seek it

out.

A network of footpaths enables you to explore some of the area on foot. Tideswell is a good centre from which to start exploring. For instance, take the road towards Tunstead and after descending into the top of Monks Dale, which is now a nature reserve, a path cuts up through the fields to Wormhill reaching the village by the church. At the southern end of the village, at GR 124729, take the path which heads south and then south-eastwards descending into Chee Dale. Follow the path downstream to Millers Dale and then take the riverside road to Litton Mill. Just before the mill turn up Tideswell Dale, beneath the grounds of Ravenstor Youth Hostel. Upon reaching the B6049 walk the last mile or so up the road into Tideswell.

17m

Foolow Cross

Brindley Memorial, Wormhill

5 The Derwent Valley

The valley of the river Derwent is one of the most pronounced features of the Peak District landscape. The river draws its water initially from the sodden peat hags of Featherbed Moss, where a fan of little streams collect to flow south-east before turning to run in the southerly direction which characterises much of its length through the Peak. The valley soon becomes deeply entrenched with green fields rising steeply towards the moors. A feature down the length of the valley as far as Chatsworth is the escarpment of gritstone rocks which outcrop on its eastern side. Their total length is around twenty miles and most can be followed on foot. From the valley these edges dominate the skyline. Now they offer sport to climbers, vantage points to visitors and photographers and an interesting linear path for ramblers.

Below Baslow, the valley widens gradually until at Rowsley it becomes even wider with the confluence of the Derwent with the waters of the Lathkill and Bradford which join the Wye a mile or so before it reaches Rowsley. The relatively soft gritstones which enabled the rocks to be eroded to form such a pronounced valley abruptly change below Matlock, where the river cuts through limestone. Here the valley becomes more of a gorge, with the sheer cliffs of High Tor and Long Tor falling steeply to the river. The area to the west of the river at Matlock Bath is riddled with ancient lead mine workings, quarries and some caves open to the public. Below Cromford, the rocks change again and the gorge is no more.

Historical Connections

The Derwent is the major river of the region. In ancient times it must have been a formidable obstacle when in flood. There is a pattern of packhorse routes and salt ways crossing the Peak, heading for Sheffield, Chesterfield and places to the east, all having to descend to and cross the Derwent. Bridges were built at an early date; the existing bridge at Baslow was built before 1500, while the predecessor of the bridge upstream at Calver was also recorded in the fifteenth century. Derwent village bridge, now re-erected at Slippery Stones, was built in the Middle Ages and it is recorded that it was repaired in 1682. Downstream, a bridge is recorded at Yorkshire Bridge in 1599 when a wooden structure was rebuilt in stone.

Proceeding downstream, Hazelford was replaced by a bridge in 1709 and it is now known as Leadmill Bridge. Beeley Bridge below Chatsworth was built in 1761 replacing Mill Bridge, then demolished. Rowsley Bridge was in need of repair by 1682 and Darley Bridge is referred to in the same year. Matlock Bridge dates from the thirteenth century although it has been rebuilt several times. Cromford Bridge dates from the sixteenth century and stands on the site where an ancient trackway crossed the river, heading for Chesterfield. Finally at Whatstandwell agreement to build a bridge was reached as early as 1390.

The crossing points became focal points and a pattern of small villages sprung up around them. A quick glance at the map highlights this: Hathersage, Grindleford, Froggatt, Curbar, Calver,

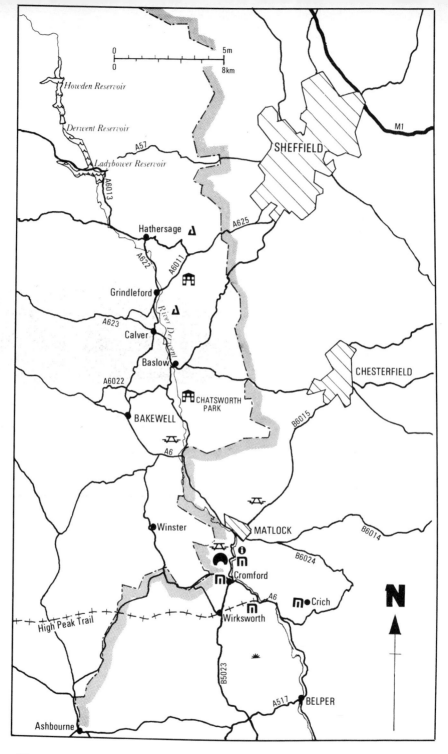

Water-cum-Jolly Dale

Monsal Dale

Chatsworth

Hathersage Church
Near the south porch is a grave, reputed to be that of Robin Hood's trusty giant, Little John.

Padley Gorge
Situated on the Longshaw Estate above Grindleford Station. The Burbage Brook descends through Padley Wood with cascades of foaming water, especially after wet weather. At Upper Padley is Padley Chapel, restored as a memorial to two Catholic priests who were captured nearby and hanged, drawn and quatered at Derby in 1588. A pilgrimage is made here on the last Thursday in July every year.

Carl Wark
Iron Age hillfort situated above Padley Gorge. Has a huge platform built of gritstone blocks up to 5ft across, and ramparts 10ft high.

Toads Mouth Rock
Curious rock formation on the Hathersage to Sheffield road, situated where the Burbage Brook crosses under the road.

The Gritstone Edges
These are an outstanding feature west of the River Derwent. Outstanding examples are Birchen Edge, Gardom's Edge, Baslow Edge, Curbar Edge, Froggatt Edge, Millstone Edge, Burbage Edge and Stanage Edge. There are paths along the tops of most of these edges and all give spectacular views. Many are popular with rock climbers. On Birchen's Edge is Nelson's Monument, erected in 1810 by a local man, while Baslow Edge has a monument to Wellington, erected in 1866. Near to Nelson's Monument are three huge rocks looking like ships with the names *Victory, Defiant,* and *Royal Soverin (sic)* on their bows. Most unusual in an area so far from the sea.

Surprise View Millstone Edge
Vantage point for looking up the valley to Castleton. Bole Hill quarry below has many abandoned millstones stacked together (and hundreds of ant hills in the quarry area).

Riverside Walk
There is a good circular path between Froggatt Bridge and Curbar Bridge on the Derwent. You can walk along one side of the river and return on the other side.

Derwent Dams
Three large reservoirs, Ladybower, Derwent and Howden, situated above the village of Bamford. Cycle hire centre at Fairholme, below Derwent Dam. There is a road up Derwent Dale on the west side of the reservoirs, but limited vehicular access above Fairholme. Footpath down eastern side of the lakes to the Ashopton viaduct on the A57. Footpath above Howden Reservoir to Slippery Stones where the packhorse bridge from the drowned Derwent village has been re-erected.

Baslow, Rowsley, Matlock, Cromford are all examples. Three villages have, however, gone. Chatsworth was demolished by the Duke of Devonshire in two stages. A new village was created at Pilsley and later Edensor was built nearer, but still out of sight of Chatsworth House. This century saw the loss of the villages of Derwent and Ashopton when the Ladybower reservoir was constructed.

The construction of the Derwent reservoirs has had a significant impact on the upper part of the valley, flooding also the Woodlands Valley which climbs up the moors towards the Snake Pass and Glossop. The Howden and Derwent dams were built together, work starting on the former in 1901 and the latter a year later. Howden was finished in 1912 but Derwent took until 1916 to complete. A village was built for the navvies employed in building the dams. It was known as Birchinlee and was situated by the present road halfway up the west side of Howden reservoir. The population rose to over 900 people and it had a shop, hospital, village hall, school and chapel. Derwent Dam found a new use during the last war for it was used by the RAF 617 squadron for practice runs before the dambusters raid on Germany and again in the film of the

raid.

Between the wars, Derwent Hall was used as a Youth Hostel and was opened by the Prince of Wales in 1932. It was built in 1672 by the Balguy family but was demolished in 1943, along with the church and village. The church spire was left standing for a few years and the east window was moved to Hathersage Church. The packhorse bridge was placed in store in 1938 and rebuilt in 1959 upstream at Slippery Stones. Ladybower reservoir was opened in 1945 by King George VI, having taken ten years to complete, and at the time it was the largest man-made lake in the country. Derwent village was situated roughly where the Mill Brook would have reached the river Derwent, and Ashopton Village was immediately adjacent Ashopton viaduct and on its south side. It is interesting that even the 1976 'Dark Peak' tourist map still showed Derwent church tower surrounded by water at GR 185886, even though it was demolished in 1947. An interesting series of photographs showing the villages and Birchinlee appear in *Bygone Days in the Peak District*. A history, with many photographs, is now available on Birchinlee, written by Brian Robinson.

Man's use of the river and its valley

does of course go back further. Its water was used to power mills, levels from mines were driven to drain them to the river and quarries have hewn stone for roads, walls, dam construction and millstones. Hundreds of unsold millstones litter the quarries of the eastern edge. Many can be seen at Millstone Edge on the A625 south east of Hathersage at GR 249799. They lie either side of an old track to Bole Hill Quarry which was reworked to supply stone to Ladybower dam.

Amongst the mills which survive several deserve mention. The largest mills are, or were, connected with the cotton industry. Calver Mill dates from 1803 and is seven stories high. The mill was used for the filming of the series 'Colditz'. At Cromford, Sir Richard Arkwright established a cotton mill in 1772, which survives in modified form on the Crich road at GR 298569. Arkwright also built Masson Mill, situated alongside the A6 between Cromford and Matlock Bath, in 1783. It is still used as a textile mill and proudly displays the legend 'Sir Richard Arkwright & Co, Established 1769'. The old cornmill on the A5012 to Newhaven situated at the edge of Cromford village has been preserved.

The Cromford Canal started close to Arkwright's first mill and the towpath makes a pleasant walk. It is joined by the now disused Cromford and High Peak Railway, which reaches the valley floor having descended the Sheep Pasture Incline from Black Rocks. Various railway buildings survive, including the wheel around which was wound the steel cable from the top of Sheep Pasture Incline. A little further along the canal is Leawood Pumphouse which has been preserved along with the Cornish-type beam engine inside it. This huge engine is steamed from time to time and is worth a visit. Details can be obtained from information offices.

In addition to the canal, there was also a railway up the valley as far as Rowsley, where it headed up the Wye at the Duke of Devonshire's insistence that Chatsworth had to be spared the intrusion of a railway. The railway exists only as far as Matlock now. Matlock formerly had a tramway and a couple of trams used to run up and down the steep hill (Bank Road) between the roundabout and Smedley's hydro, now the County Council Offices. The tramway was closed down in 1927 and the tram shelter which stood on the site of the roundabout was moved to the adjacent gardens where it can still be seen.

Matlock developed as a spa town and many hydros, or more correctly hydropathic establishments, were built in the mid-nineteenth century. The last major hydro to survive was Smedleys, which finally closed its doors in 1955. It is a massive structure and is worth having a look at. It is now the County Council Offices and was built by John Smedley who also built Riber Castle which dominates the skyline to the south of the town. The castle's huge structure cost him £60,000 and is now a fauna reserve of British and European animals and birds.

The Derwent Today
Despite the urbanisation of parts of the valley, there is still much to see which will interest the visitor. The reservoirs have a beauty of their own, and the dams are particularly impressive when overflowing, particularly the Derwent Dam. Unfortunately the woods which surround the upper two reservoirs add little harmony to the scene, for they are stark and emphasise a heavy shoreline, particularly when the water level drops.

Nonetheless, the road from Ashopton Viaduct is worth taking to the top of Howden reservoir. It finishes at a cul-de-sac where there is a path which leads the short distance to Slippery Stones where the Derwent village packhorse bridge was rebuilt in 1959.

On Sundays and Bank Holiday Mondays between Easter and the end of October, visitors must park at Fairholmes, near Derwent Dam (except cars displaying a disabled person's orange disc). To get further up the valley, you must walk, hire a bike or catch the regular minibus service.

Some four miles below Ladybower reservoir is Hathersage. It has associations with Charlotte Brontë who wove her novel *Jane Eyre* around the area, calling the town Morton. In the churchyard is the gravestone of Little John, the friend and companion of Robin Hood. Apparently he was a native of Hathersage, known as John

---

PLACES OF INTEREST NEAR CROMFORD

Cromford
A fascinating village which may be explored with the aid of the Arkwright Society's leaflet, available in most bookshops in the area.

Arkwright's Cromford Mill, Mill Lane, Cromford
Sir Richard Arkwright's original mill now being developed into a museum. Another Arkwright mill is Masson Mill, which can be seen (exterior only) alongside the A6 between Matlock Bath and Cromford.

Leawood Pumping Station, Cromford
Old pumping station used to pump water from the river Derwent to the Cromford Canal. Fully restored and preserved in the engine house is a 50in Cornish-type beam engine which is steamed periodically.

Cromford Canal
Horse-drawn boat trips from Cromford Wharf. Interesting buildings at the foot of the Sheep Pasture Incline of the Cromford and High Peak Railway, with railway-canal trans-shipment point. Pleasant walks along the towpath.

Cromford Bridge
A fifteenth-century bridge with rounded arches one side, pointed arches the other! At the Cromford end is an early eighteenth-century fishing temple, almost identical to Walton and Cotton's in Beresford Dale, and the ruins of a bridge chapel. On the parapet of the bridge a cryptic inscription records the successful leaping of the parapet by a horse and rider in 1697.

Lea Rhododendron Gardens, Lea
Five hundred varieties of rhododendrons and azaleas set in a five-acre garden. Many are unusual and mature specimens. In May and June the garden is a riot of colour and is highly recommended. Plants available.

Tramway Museum, Crich
National collection of trams. In addition to an exhibition there is also over a mile of track and your entrance ticket includes a tram ride.

Little and made his living as a nailer until he found everlasting fame. The town has a passenger railway station on the line between Sheffield and Manchester which also has stations at Grindleford, Bamford, Hope and Edale.

South of the town the Burbage Brook flows through Padley Wood to join the Derwent at Grindleford. The descent of the brook through the wood is steep and the brook rushes amid boulders and trees in a steep sided valley. It is a beauty spot missed by many visitors who overlook it. It is best visited by walking upstream to get the best views of the rushing white water. By a bus stop on the B6521, immediately above Grindleford Station is a stile which gives access to the wood. The path is easy to follow and upon passing through a gate, drops down a series of steps to a footbridge. Once over the brook, the path climbs steeply to an elevated level above the stream. Eventually the path leaves the wood and crosses through flat fields to reach the A625. Ahead lies Stanage Edge, and by the main road Toad's Mouth Rock, a curious natural rock formation overlooked by Carl Wark, a hillfort of the Iron Age. To the south is the Longshaw Estate, purchased from the Duke of Rutland by subscription and given to the National Trust when he sold his 11,500 acre estate here in 1927. A path returns to Grindleford through the estate, past the

Carl Wark and Higger Tor from Padley Gorge

Stanage Edge

PLACES OF INTEREST AROUND THE DERWENT VALLEY

Chatsworth Estate Farm Shop, Pilsley
Available for the sale of estate produce, including game when in season.

Chatsworth House, near Baslow
Known as the Palace of the Peak, with one of the finest private collections of art and antiques in Britain. The gardens are renowned for the Emperor Fountain and the Cascades, the Azalea Dell, and the formal gardens with its Laburnam Tunnel.

Near the house is a farmyard/forestry exhibtion. Here is a ten-ton pile of timber, representing just 24 hour's growth of timber on the estate's 2,500 acres of woodland.

At Carlton Lees, adjacent to the car park at the southern entrance to Chatsworth Park, the estate has opened a large garden centre.

Many walks in Stand Wood (leaflet available).

Baslow
At the northern end of the village there is a fine medieval stone bridge with a very small guard house just large enough for one person to collect tolls. The church clock has VICTORIA 1897 instead of numerals, while inside is a dog-whip used to chase stray dogs out during church services.

Calver Mill and Calver Craft Centre
Former textile mill, built by Arkwright in 1803-4, used in the television series 'Colditz', but not open to the public. The fine eighteenth-century stone bridge has been by-passed in recent years by a modern structure. Nearby craft centre, bookshop and cafeteria.

Edensor
An attractive estate village built during 1838-42 by Joseph Paxton to house the inhabitants of the original village, which the sixth Duke of Devonshire considered spoilt the view from Chatsworth House. Nearby Pilsley, also a Chatsworth estate village, extended by Paxton to house some of the other villagers. Each of the houses in Edensor are of a different architectural style.

Caudwell's Mill, Rowsley
Water driven flour mill. Guided tours available.

house and its lake. Longshaw is the site for the Longshaw Sheepdog Trial held every September. There is a Natioanl Trust Information Centre, shop and cafeteria at Longshaw.

The gritstone edges which are a feature of the upper Derwent offer the opportunity for a marvellous walk for some fifteen miles, from the singposted path by a stile on the Baslow side of the Robin Hood Inn on the A619 (GR 277722). The path cuts around Gardom's Edge and then crosses the A621 heading for Wellington's Monument. From here, it follows Baslow, Froggatt and Curbar Edges, passing a small stone circle by Froggatt Edge. The views along the edges down into the Derwent Valley and across to Eyam Moor and Longstone Moor are

15m

marvellous. It is difficult to appreciate that the outskirts of Sheffield are only four to five miles away. A footpath to Nether Padley brings one to Padley Gorge and the climb back on to Stanage Edge which winds around to Moscar above Bamford Moor and Ladybower.

Below Longshaw lie the villages of Calver and Baslow, so close that they almost merge into each other. Part of Calver by the traffic lights is actually known as Calver Sough and takes its name from an old lead mine in the area, last worked in the mid-nineteenth century when a steam pumping engine was erected close to the cross-roads. Just to the north of Calver is Stoke Hall. After being empty for some time, this

Guard house, Baslow Bridge

Baslow Bridge

beautiful building has been converted to a hotel and its future is now assured. There is an attractive walk between Froggatt and Calver bridges. A path follows each side of the river and makes a good circular walk. It is easier to park near Calver bridge than at Froggatt. The river is deep, wide and slow moving and the broad expanse of water looks very attractive on a sunny day. Baslow perhaps is a little more interesting than Calver, with its little shops set around a green at Nether End. Beyond the impressive Cavendish Hotel, is a car park. If you prefer a walk to Chatsworth, rather than driving there, then park here. Cross the little brook a few yards eastwards from the car park and take the signposted path down the brookside past a rare sight in this area — a thatched cottage. The path crosses the river meadows and reaches Chatsworth by Queen Mary's Bower and the elegant bridge over the river.

Chatsworth, the home of the Cavendish family, is one of the Wonders of the Peak, and one of the finest houses in Britain. The son of William Cavendish and Bess of Hardwick was created first Earl of Devonshire, and his descendant, the fourth Earl, was created the first Duke of Devonshire for supporting the cause of William of Orange. Bess of Hardwick brought considerable wealth to the Cavendish family and with the dissolution of the monasteries, this wealth was used to purchase land on a large scale throughout the Peak District and elsewhere. The wealth from landed property was augmented, chiefly during the eighteenth century, by considerable royalties from lead mines in the Peak District and also from copper ores obtained from the Duke's mine at Ecton in the Manifold Valley. In fact between 1760 and 1817, the Ecton mine alone

produced an estimated profit of £335,000, and this enormous income created a dynasty of extremely wealthy men. As a consequence, Chatsworth is a treasure house, richly endowed with old masters, priceless furniture, tapestries, carvings and porcelain.

Today it is open to visitors and the route taken through the house includes the majority of the main state rooms on the south front. Much of the present house was built by the first and sixth Dukes, ie in the seventeenth century and in the early part of the nineteenth century. It therefore makes an interesting comparison with the older Haddon Hall. Perhaps one of the most fortunate aspects of Chatsworth is that a considerable number of the treasures are on display. Everywhere one goes in the house there are priceless and beautiful works of art. You should allow plenty of time for a walk around Chatsworth, for there is so much that otherwise will be missed. For instance, the wood and alabaster carvings in the chapel and the painting of the violin in the music room. At the end of the tour there is now a shop in the former orangery which leads out into the garden.

The garden is also worthy of a visit. In fact, it should be given at least half a day of your time in order to explore the various points of interest. It includes the Emperor Fountain which is set in its canal pond and is noted for being the highest gravity fed fountain in the world, although seldom seen at its full height of 260ft. Elsewhere in the gardens can be seen the maze, set on the site of what used to be the conservatory built by Paxton and a forerunner of his Crystal Palace which was built in London for the Great Exhibition of 1851. Behind the house are the cascades and the aqueduct, together with Stand Wood with its various footpaths along the valley side.

Chatsworth House and Stand Woods

Above the wood stands the prospect tower, a relic of the Elizabethan manor house that existed here before the present house was built. A more recent innovation has been the development of a forestry and farming display plus an adventure playground which are always a special treat for children. There are no lions and safari parks here which is a saving grace. There are however several festivals at different times of the year, details of which are given in the gazetteer and which can add immensely to a visit to this wonderful place.

If you like to ramble do not overlook Chatsworth Park. There are several private paths through the park to which the public are permitted access and these are shown on notice boards. If you are south of the house itself, whether on foot or even in the car, look out for the deer on the east bank of the river. At the southern end of the park, close to One Arch Bridge (now with traffic lights) is Carlton Lees picnic area and car park set amid the trees above the road. It is a useful place to park if exploring the estate paths and a plaque indicates the paths. There is a tea bar and the estate sells a leaflet about its Stand Wood walks which take you above and behind Chatsworth House. Recently opened is the Chatsworth garden centre just beyond the car park.

Downstream from Chatsworth is Beeley, then Rowsley and beyond it the

Heights of Abraham

Two show caves and the Victoria Prospect Tower. The caves are the Great Rutland Cavern and Nestors Mine, and the Great Masson Cavern. Both of these are part of a considerable complex of old lead mines situated beneath Masson Hill. Access to the Heights of Abraham can now be obtained by taking the cable car from just upstream of Matlock Bath railway station. It should be noted that the cars do not actually stop at the cable car stations, but proceed *very* slowly.

The Royal Cave

Situated adjacent to Gulliver's Kingdom.

Gulliver's Kingdom, Temple Walk

Model village, amusements and children's fantasy land.

High Tor Grounds

Sixty acres of grounds with walks and views into the Derwent Valley with the river nearly 400ft below. There is

a café and bar on the site. Access from Matlock Bath: (just up river from the railway station), from Dale Road or Church Street, Matlock, or from Starkholmes.

Temple Mine

An old lead mine converted into a tourist attraction. Details from the Peak District Lead Mining Museum.

Peak District Lead Mining Museum, The Pavilion

A museum dealing with the history, traditions and techniques of an ancient industry. Central exhibit is a huge water-pressure engine built in 1819 and brought from a lead mine at Winster.

Riber Castle Wildlife Park, Matlock

A collection of European birds and animals, including several rare species. The castle, which dominates the skyline for miles, was built by John Smedley, who owned Smedley's Hydro (now the County Council Offices) in Matlock.

urbanised sprawl of Matlock's suburbs. Without doubt, it is Matlock Bath which is the mecca for many visitors to this area. The A6 becomes choked with cars on sunny Bank Holidays. Not surprisingly, there is much to see, so allow plenty of time and a full wallet. One of the more recent additions is the Mining Museum, run by the Peak District Mines Historical Society. The centre piece of its exhibits is a huge water-pressure engine found in a mine at Winster. This is an interesting, not a stuffy museum, and

while you interest yourself in the exhibits, children can explore simulated passages and shafts. A dramatic addition to the attractions at Matlock Bath opened at Easter 1984. Now it is possible to take a cable car up to the Heights of Abraham. This gives a spectacular and unique view of the Derwent Valley. The cable car station is a little upstream of Matlock Bath Railway Station. It is easy to locate by looking for the cables slung over the A6 and the river Derwent. Elsewhere in the town there is Gulliver's

Kingdom and there are several show caves and mines. The Rutland Mine has a very good display and the Mining Museum has opened the old Temple Mine for visitors too. There are a good range of shops, a promenade above the river and a railway station. Each year, Matlock Bath has its illuminations with illuminated floats on the river and a firework display. More details on dates can be obtained from the information office next to the Mining Museum.

Just south of the town is the New Bath Hotel. Most people tend to regard it as being purely residential, but it is not. When you begin to flag a little from

'doing the rounds' in Matlock Bath, it is an excellent choice for coffee and biscuits. Matlock itself is a good shopping centre, but it lacks the architectural appeal of Buxton, Bakewell or Ashbourne, for example. Fortunately its shops are on the flat, for much of the town itself overlooks the river.

Beyond the Matlocks lies Cromford which grew as a result of the prosperous mill of Sir Richard Arkwright. Arkwright built the Greyhound Inn together with houses for his workers and a school for their children. North Street, on the south side of the road to

Greyhound Hotel, Cromford

Waterwheel, Water Lane, Cromford

Wirksworth was built by him and the school is situated at the end of the street. Behind the Wirksworth road and just to the east of North Street is the village lock up and the 'tail' or beginning of Cromford Sough. The water is piped across the A6 and was used to supply water to Arkwright's Mill, crossing Mill Lane by the mill on a cast iron aqueduct dated 1821, and to the Cromford Canal.

Mill Lane is the road to Crich which is also of interest. After passing under the 1821 aqueduct and by the side of the canal basin it passes the church built by Arkwright. If you look back across the basin, you can see Rock House where he lived. Across the old bridge with its little chapel remains and fishing house is the entrance to Willersley Castle. Now a Methodist guest house it was built by Arkwright but he died in 1792 prior to its completion. The road keeps close to the river before turning towards Lea Bridge and Holloway. The latter was the home of Florence Nightingale, who lived at Lea Hurst, now an old folks' home, but occasionally it may be visited on open days. A few years ago a firm of

Cromford Church

River Derwent at Cromford

Bakewell solicitors opened a long forgotten box and were intrigued to find it contained some of her possessions. Lea was also the home of Alison Uttley who was born at Castle Top Farm.When the rhododendrons are in flower in May and June it is worth visiting Lea Rhododendron Gardens. An old quarry was planted with timber and rhododendrons about fifty years ago. Today the different species of rhododendrons are mature and a truely wonderful sight. The scent of the flowers pervades the whole wood and the colours in the flowers left the author amazed by their variety and beauty.

The road up the hill at Holloway affords some good views over the Derwent Valley towards the white painted Alderwasley Hall. Just beyond the double bend at Wakebridge, in a clump of young trees on the west side of the road, look for the wooden headstocks of Jingler Lead Mine. They are the last of their kind to survive in Derbyshire. Another mile or so brings one to the outskirts of Crich and the tramway museum with its national collection of trams. There are over forty vehicles including a handful from overseas. They vary from a horse-drawn Sheffield tram of 1874 to another Sheffield tram of 1950, which was the city's last tram when the service finished in 1960. Your car park ticket entitles you to ride on one of the selection of trams which are operated on the mile or so of track down the edge of a quarry and beneath Crich Stand, a monument to the Sherwood Foresters who fell in the two world wars.

A trip to Crich can usefully be left for a rainy day for there is much to see and much can be done even when it rains. The tram sheds can be visited as well as a museum which is housed behind the facade of the old Derby Assembly Rooms. With much Victoriana preserved in a street scene, you can lose yourself in a past age and wonder how long it must be before the price of oil causes a tramway revival.

When you take your tramride, look out for the lead mining display erected by the Peak District Mines Historical Society. You can get off to look at this and get another tram back. Lead ore was smelted in the area of course, initially in bole hearths which required wind for draught and later in cupolas which were an early reverberatory furnace. One such cupola existed at Stone Edge about 9 miles due north of Crich at GR 334669. The chimney still stands and it is the oldest free standing industrial chimney in the country, dating from about 1770.

6 The Dark Peak

North of the limestone lies the Dark Peak. It is really an unfortunate description, for it connotes a forboding area whereas much of it is not. Indeed, the gritstone regions which surround the limestone include some of the best scenery in the area, whether it be around the upper Dane, the Churnet, Stanage or the northern area under discussion. In fact, many will incline to the view that the Dark Peak is of more interest than the flatter limestone district further south. In addition to the great expanse of peat moors such as Kinder Scout and Bleaklow, there are the less rigorous walking areas of the Hope and Edale valleys separated by the ridge between Lose Hill and Mam Tor, with the

isolated Win Hill situated at the end of Hope Valley and blocking the east-west trend of the Edale Valley. Here can be seen some of the best countryside that the Peak has to offer.

To the south lies Bradwell at the neck of a valley between the somewhat featureless Bradwell Moor and Bradwell Edge which dominates the village. Beyond is Abney Moor and Eyam Edge where the gritstones drop steeply to the limestones and the White Peak.

Historical Connections
This is an area of significant historical interest. The hillfort on Mam Tor commands an impressive position and sits astride a routeway possibly as old as

Mam Tor

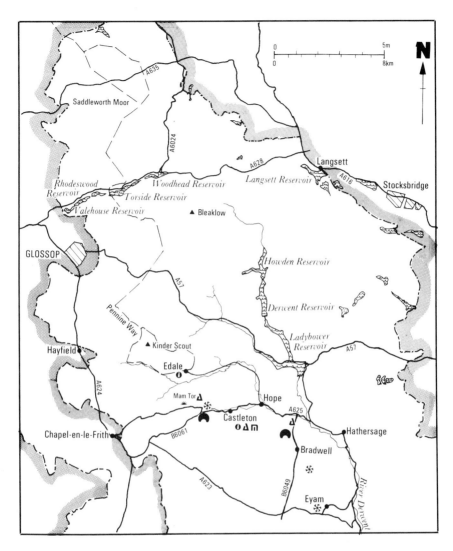

the earliest colonisation of the Peak. The
Romans established a fort at *Navio,* near
Brough north-west of Bradwell. Their
roads stretched away from Buxton,
along Doctor's Gate to Ardotalia and
eastwards towards Sheffield. Relics of
their occupation can be seen in Buxton
Museum. Later, a Norman castle was
built nearby, giving its name to the
settlement below it — Castleton. The
keep still survives, together with much of
its perimeter wall. All around are the

relics of the once important lead mining
industry and hundreds of shafts
pockmark the landscape. Beneath Mam
Tor is the Odin Mine, traditionally said
to have been worked by the Saxons.
There is no evidence to prove this, but it
all helps to create the impression of
antiquity in the area.

On the moors, the early lines of
communication have remained relatively
intact, especially the possible Roman
road known as Doctor's Gate. Whatever

113

its age, this narrow track is an amazing relic and a watchful eye needs to be kept to ensure its preservation. The track is actually named after Dr John Talbot, an illegitimate son of the Earl of Shrewsbury who was the vicar of Glossop from 1494 until 1550. Presumably he would have used the road when travelling from his home to his father's castle at Sheffield. The track is three to five feet wide and can be seen to advantage on Coldharbour Moor, where the original paving slabs and kerbstones are intact.

Further Roman roads can be traced in this area such as the road from *Aquae Arnemetiae* to *Ardotalia* (Buxton to Glossop) and a good account of them is given in *Peakland Roads and Trackways* by A.E. and E.M. Dodd. Of more recent origin are the numerous packhorse routes which cross the area, many making useful footpaths such as the Edale to Castleton path via Hollins Cross which can be traced on the OS map in its entirety. Alternatively northwest of Hope Cross the Roman Road, which is now a bridle path, crosses Blackley Clough where other hollow ways can be seen, now completely disused, but worn down over centuries of use. Our legacy of these old roadways is an important network of paths which enable us to explore the area thoroughly.

Of equal interest are the remains of early settlements. There is little to see at the Roman forts of *Navio* at Brough and *Ardotalia* at Glossop (erroneously referred to by the ficticious name of Melandra). Mam Tor's Iron Age fort, apparently built around the fifth century BC is more interesting. Its dominating position above the impregnable south facing cliff of Mam Tor is impressive in itself, with magnificent views down the valleys. For the curious, however, the ramparts on the western and northern slopes still remain. You can park close to the fort at the car park on the Edale-Castleton road at Rushop Edge (GR 124833). Mam Tor and the Winnats form part of the National Trust's 30,000 acre High Peak Estate, which also includes much of the 'Dark Peak'.

Below Mam Tor sits Castleton, on an outpost of limestone worked for centuries for lead and Blue John stone and now for cement. Above the village is its castle on a site reminiscent of Mam Tor with its sheer drop and protected flank. The sheer drop is to Cave Dale which perhaps gives the most impressive view of the castle keep, looking across the dry valley. The alternative view, of course, is from the village, but this lacks a degree of perspective, having to view it from below. The castle was built by William Peveril, the illegitimate son of William the Conqueror, in 1080, as a wooden stockade. This was later rebuilt in stone and the stone keep was added in 1175. The castle was only one of several in the Peak, others existing at Bakewell, Ashford-in-the-Water, Hathersage and possibly Pilsbury, north of Hartington, but these were minor affairs and Peveril Castle was by far the most important. It seems to have been a hunting lodge of the Royal Forest of the High Peak and Henry II happened to be here when he received the submission of King Malcolm of Scotland in 1157.

Castleton and its Caves

For the historian, or even the curious, there is much to commend Castleton and it is easy to spend a day in the area. Even in bad weather, it is possible to avoid the rain by going underground in one of the four show caves or visiting the various shops, the church, information centre and museum (the Ollerenshaw Collection) in the village. Let us start however with the caves. Only one is a true cave — Peak Cavern, which is owned by the Duchy of Lancaster. It used to be known as the Devil's Arse but such vulgarity did not survive Victorian sensitivity. The cave system is very extensive, far more so than the portion open to the visitor. From its mouth flows the Peakshole Water, which originates as a number of streams flowing off the moor above. The cave entrance was, until the last ropemaker died a few years ago, used for making ropes and the rope walk can still be seen. Gone, however, are the little ropemakers' cottages which used to stand within the entrance to the cave itself. The ropes were made for centuries and Castleton brides used to be presented with a locally-made washing line.

Three more show caves, or more strictly speaking mines with natural caves in them, exist at Treak Cliff below Mam Tor. On Treak Cliff itself, are Blue John Mine and Treak Cliff Cavern. The former is a mine for Blue John stone, much favoured by the Victorians for decoration. The purplish stone is a variety of fluorspar that has been impregnated with hydrocarbons. The main veins have been exploited now, creating beautiful vases and inlay work. Chatsworth has the largest turned vase from a single piece of stone and Kedleston Hall near to Derby has much inlay work. There is a good display of the stone, both in turned work and in cross sections in Buxton Museum. Nowadays only about one third of a ton a year is mined, for costume jewellery. The age of the workings is unknown but it is unlikely to be more than two or three hundred years. Anything older is sheer speculation. Pompeii revealed vases in stone similar to Blue John but it

PLACES OF INTEREST AROUND CASTLETON

Peveril Castle
Norman castle of which the keep and part of the retaining wall remains. Situated high above the village.

Cave Dale and the Winnats
Two deep and spectacular dry gorges near to Castleton. Cave Dale is approached from a footpath just off the Market Place. The Winnats Pass is larger and deeper and carries the old road to Whaley Bridge.

Mam Tor
A pronounced hill situated above Castleton known as the 'Shivering Mountain' because of its vertical face which is prone to rock falls and landslips. Surmounted by an Iron Age hillfort which still retains its pronounced ditch.

Ollerenshaw Collection
A small museum with a fine collection of Blue John Stone, situated in Cross Street, Castleton.

Odin Lead Mine
The Peak District's oldest recorded lead mine and one of the richest. There is the remains of a crushing mill just below the road below Mam Tor.

Castleton's Caves
There are several caves around Castleton open to the public:
Blue John Cavern, Mam Tor. Old mine-workings for Blue John stone. The largest range of caverns containing veins of the stone.
Treak Cliff Cavern. Part natural and part an old mine for Blue John stone. Contains some attractive stalactites and stalagmites.
Speedwell Cavern, Winnats Pass. An old lead mine where visitors travel by boat on an underground canal.
Peak Cavern, Castleton Village. A large cave system of which part is open to the public. The entrance used to be used for the manufacture of ropes, and the ropewalk still survives.
Bagshawe Cavern, Bradwell. A show cave with an adventure trip, the latter by appointment only.

has now been proved that this stone came from the Middle East not Castleton.

Blue John mine descends steeply with countless steps to the bottom, which can be slippery in wet weather so ensure you wear suitable footwear. Treak Cliff Cavern includes some rather fine grottoes of stalactites and stalagmites which were discovered during a search for fresh veins of Blue John stone in 1926. The Speedwell Mine is advertised as being a unique experience — the only mine where visitors are conducted underground by boat. The mine was designed like this in 1774. The man behind the scheme was John Gilbert, the agent to the Duke of Bridgewater and the man who introduced the Duke to James Brindley. The Bridgewater Canal actually went underground to a boat loading wharf near the coal face at Worsley. John Gilbert was a partner in a copper mine at Ecton adjacent to the Duke of Devonshire's famous Ecton Mine and an underground canal was

introduced at Ecton in 1767.
Unfortunately the Speedwell Mine was
uneconomic, in contrast to the Ecton
and Worsley mines, and soon closed.

The adjacent Winnats Pass is
spectacular. It is thought to have been
eroded when it was under the sea rather
than been a former cave system. It is
closed to heavy traffic but whether on
foot, car or bike it is worth seeing. It is
used to be the main turnpike road until
the latter was re-routed under Mam Tor
because the gradient was easier.
Unfortunately the face of Mam Tor is
continually eroding due to hard bands of
gritstone lying on softer shale. This has
given rise to the name 'Shivering
Mountain' but sometimes the movement
is more severe, resulting in landslips that
affect the road, causing subsidence on a
large scale. The road is now permanently
closed and has been abandoned
completely. The Winnats could be the

alternative route again but the preferred
route is a much more expensive proposal
going much further south across
Bradwell Moor. Meanwhile cars can use
the Winnats Pass road, but should
negotiate it with care, especially when it
is icy. Heavy traffic must divert via
Bradwell and Peak Forest.

Under Treak Cliff is the Odin Mine,
which was worked for lead and not Blue
John. Although its name implies a
Saxon connection, there is no evidence
of it being worked prior to the
seventeenth century. Its main interest to
the visitor is the crushing circle which
survives on the east side of the road just
above the Treak Cliff Cavern. The main
entrance to the mine was lost during
road widening operations and although
the large opening west of the road does
lead into the workings these are
dangerous and should not be entered.
The crushing circle consists of a cast-

iron track upon which lead ore would be heaped. This was then crushed by the millstone (of 5ft 10in diameter) which would be rolled around a pivot by a horse. The millstone with its circular iron tyre also survives, and it is an interesting relic of this bygone era and industry. The old mine tips are also a useful place to get out of the car and photograph the upper end of the Hope Valley and Castleton village itself.

If you do not feel energetic enough to visit the caves you can see the products of Blue John in the village gift shops and also visit the Ollerenshaw Collection of Blue John wares. The information centre has a display on lead mining, while a few yards away are the old hall (now a youth hostel) and the church, noted for its collection of old books which include a 1593 Cranmer Bible and a Breeches Bible.

The Castleton garland ceremony attracts a lot of interest on the evening of 29 May. The Garland King and his lady proceed on horseback through the village. The king carries a 60lb frame around him which is bedecked with flowers. The procession stops at each of the six inns in the village and eventually the garland is hoisted to hang from one of the pinnacles of the church tower, after the top bunch of flowers have been formally placed on the war memorial. It is pleasant to witness such ancient ceremonies, surviving in our modern age.

The Plague Village and Abney

Eyam is another village steeped in history and interest. It is perhaps most well known because of the tenacity of its villagers when stricken by the plague in 1665. The story is well documented elsewhere but briefly, the disease reached the village in a consignment of cloth sent from London. Encouraged by

their vicar, the villagers decided to cut themselves off from the outside world and although the disease abated during the cold winter months it returned with ferocious consequences in the summer of 1666. In all a total of 257 villagers died. Today one can see the Plague Cottage where it all started, on the main road just west of the church. The grassy area to the left of the cottages is the site of the old village pond and nearby the village stocks still survive.

In the churchyard are graves to the plague victims including Catherine Mompesson, the wife of the vicar. William Mompesson acted as leader, comforter and liaison officier with the outside world but was not spared the life of his wife. She lies buried near to the village cross. The Celtic cross should not be missed. Although not complete, it is a remarkable survivor, perhaps all the more striking because the cross head survives on top of the shaft together with its intricate carving. Beyond the church one can find graves of plague victims who were buried in makeshift graves, perhaps to maintain family isolation, or when the graveyard reached its capacity. It makes one wonder how many lie in unmarked resting places beyond the churchyard wall. Look for the Hancock graves and the Talbot family graves in the family orchard at Riley House Farm, but please ensure that you do not trespass. Church services were held in the open during the time of the plague at Cucklet Delf and a service of remembrance is held there annually.

One of the main aspects of village life has been the local mining industry. The Glebe Mines are situated in the village and the headstocks of the shaft are clearly visible from the road at the top of Eyam Dale. The exploitation of lead ore, once paramount, is now secondary to fluorspar but at the time of writing the

PLACES OF INTEREST IN AND NEAR EYAM

Plague Cottages

A group of cottages in the centre of Eyam, where the plague arrived in a box of cloth from London in 1665. Two-thirds of the villagers died as a result. This interesting village has a bull ring where bull baiting took place, opposite the fine hall built after the plague, and village stocks.

Riley Graves

East of the village off the Grindleford road, the graves of the Hancock family, who died in the plague.

Mompesson's Well

North of the village on the road to Sir William Hill. One of the places where food was left for the villagers during their voluntary isolation at the time of the plague.

Eyam Moor Open moorland with Bronze Age tumuli and stone circles

A narrow rocky valley south of Eyam, where open-air church services wereheld at the time of the plague, to reduce the risk of infection. A remembrance service is held here on the last Sunday in August every year.

Eyam Church

Graves of many of the plague victims, including Catherine Mompesson, the vicar's wife. Also in the churchyard is an outstanding carved Saxon Cross, the only one in the Midlands with head complete.

In the church is Mompesson's chair, dated 1665, while in the well outside is a sundial which not only gives astrononmical data but also gives the time in different parts of the world.

mine, along with its associate Ladywash Mine on Eyam Edge, has been on a care and maintenance basis for several years. Although Eyam Edge looks peaceful now and at first glance shows little sign of lead mining activities, this is very deceptive. The area has seen intense working over three centuries and even after most of the mines closed much of the tips were reworked for their fluorspar content. Glebe Mine is very old and is now only used as an airshaft to Ladywash Mine.

Today Eyam is a small and attractive village nestling under Eyam Edge. It has several interesting streets with some fine properties and an attractive hall near to the church, completed in 1676. On the

hillside above the village sits Beech Hurst, an attractive house now converted into a Youth Hostel. Eyam Edge affords some good panoramic views marred perhaps by the fluorspar treatment plant of Laportes at Cavendish Mill situated across Middleton Dale. It is nonetheless a salutary reminder that these beautiful places also have to sustain work to maintain the fabric of the area, whether we like the consequences of this or not. It comes as no surprise that from time to time the planning authority comes into conflict with industry; quarrying and mining operations present a continual problem in this conservation-conscious era. Laportes process a very fine quality fluorspar from their mine, Sallet Hole No 2, on Longstone Edge and from opencast workings on Longshore Edge and Bradwell Moor, plus spar from other 'tributors' in the area.

Behind Eyam village, the ground rises to Eyam Moor, with its numerous cairns and stone circle. This high ground stretches northwards towards the Hope and Derwent Valleys and westwards to Great Hucklow where it is known as Abney Moor. The Bretton Brook cuts a big slice out of the moor and it drains the area to the north-west. The whole area is like a huge island, of about ten square miles in extent, surrounded by edges and steeply descending ground. It is an area often neglected by tourists, yet the Great Hucklow to Hathersage road cuts right across the area. There are some good views across Eyam Moor from the road which runs past the gliding club at Camphill Farm, through the tiny village of Abney and also past

Highlow Hall. The latter is not a contradiction in terms in the Peak, for 'low' is a very common Derbyshire word meaning 'burial mound' or 'burial hill'. The hall was the home of the Eyre family and is one of several sixteenth-century houses in the area. Offerton Hall to the north-west and Hazlebadge Hall south of Bradwell are other examples.

This moorland area has some good footpaths which enable you to explore it even better. A good circular route of about ten miles gives a good impression of the area. Foolow makes a convenient starting point. It is a small but interesting village complete with its village green, pond and cross. Look out for the seventeenth-century hall and the manor house. The cross was possibly a boundary marker of the Royal Forest of the Peak. Take the Bretton road out of the village for about half a mile and then take the path to Abney Grange, first ascending Eyam Edge. Descend into

10m

Plague Cottages, Eyam

Bretton Clough to cross the Bretton Brook and climb up to Abney Grange. Turn west at the grange and upon reaching the Hucklow Edge to Abney road cross the road and Abney Moor to the junction of two lanes near Robin Hood's Cross of which only the base remains. It is probably a boundary cross, although it is also at the crossing of packhorse routes from Brough and Bradwell. At the junction bear right and proceed north-east along Shatton Lane around Shatton Edge. Descend some distance towards Shatton village before taking a path off to the right which leads roughly eastwards towards Offerton Hall. It nestles under Offerton Moor overlooking Hathersage with a fine view towards the moors which separate the Derwent Valley from Sheffield.

From Offerton Hall take the track to Highlow Hall rounding Offerton Moor and dropping down into the wooded Dunge Brook. Nearby is Robin Hood's Stoop (possibly a further cross base) from which (legend has it) he fired an arrow into Hathersage Churchyard; a remarkable feat as the church must be 1½ miles away! Hathersage, of course, was the home of Little John who is buried in the churchyard. From here take the Abney road and opposite the drive to The Oaks drop down into the valley of Highlow Brook to Stoke Ford. Here Abney Clough meets Bretton Clough and the path crosses a footbridge and climbs up the east side of Bretton Clough. A well defined track crosses Eyam Moor heading for Mag Clough where it reaches the road across Sir William Hill from Great Hucklow to Grindleford. Take the Eyam road, where on the right can be seen the headgear of Ladywash Mine recently worked by Laporte Industries. The road passes Mompesson's Well, named after William Mompesson, the rector of Eyam during

the plague of 1665-6. At this time the village cut itself off from the outside world to contain the disease and arranged for food to be left at certain points around the village. This is one of the places.

There is also a barn near here just through a gate on the left. It is the former engine house to New Engine Mine; reputed to be the deepest lead mine shaft in Derbyshire at over 1,000ft deep. Unfortunately, the chimney became dangerous and was recently demolished. Pass the Youth Hostel at Beech Hurst and descend the road into the village. From Eyam, there is a choice of routes back to

Eyam Cross

121

Foolow. Either take the road or the path through the fields just to the south of the road which is more pleasant and slightly more direct. If the climb out of Foolow, up the side of Eyam Edge, is too strenuous, start from the top of Eyam Edge and ignore Eyam village by turning right upon reaching the road across Sir William Hill.

From Bradwell to Edale

Before leaving this area for the Edale Valley one must not forget Bradwell, nestling at the north end of Bradford Dale. It grew as a mining community and it retains that character. It used to be famous for the hard hats made there which the miners used and which were known as 'Bradder Beavers'.

There are few 'attractions' here for the tourist except for Bagshawe Cavern. The cave is reached by descending a flight of ninety-eight steps through an old lead mine. The show cave is half a mile in length past beautiful formations and other items of interest. Also a more adventurous caving trip is available. Mention has been made that old caves and mines should only be entered with an experienced guide. Here is one of the best with a guide included for a reasonable fee. This introduction to caving involves chimney climbing, ladderwork and crawling. The adventure trip, as it is known, needs to be booked in advance and you have to take at least a hand torch, strong shoes and old clothes. The address is given at the rear of this book. At the time of writing the cave management claim a 100 per cent accident-free record.

Nearby is Hope with its ancient church, with a fourteenth-century broach-spire which is unusual in the Peak District. The rest of the church is much later, but there are one or two interesting features such as a Saxon cross shaft in the churchyard and two fonts, one of the twelfth century and another of 1662 which was brought from

Eyam Church

Derwent Church when the latter was demolished to make way for Ladybower Reservoir. Dominating the landscape behind the village are the twin hills of Lose Hill and Win Hill. Between the two hills flows the river Noe to join the Peakshole Water at Hope village. This narrow valley carries the river together with the road and railway line to Edale. After two or three miles the valley turns westwards and opens out considerably. Here is the Vale of Edale in which the tiny village of Edale nestles under Kinder Scout. The peacefulness of this little valley is often ruptured in summer, but the tranquillity often returns in winter particularly under

Bretton Clough

a blanket of snow.

To the south of the valley is the ridge that runs from Lose Hill via Mam Tor to Lords Seat on Rushop Edge. Along the ridge runs a footpath which is an old packhorse route running from Chapel-en-le-Frith via Mam Tor and Hollins Cross to Hope and onwards through Hathersage to Sheffield. Today this is a marvellous footpath which can be used as part of a circular route based on Castleton. From the Market Place in Castleton, take the path up Cave Dale to where it reaches an old green lane between Dirtlow Rake and Eldon Hill. Bear north-west along the old Portway which heads for Mam Tor Hill Fort. From here take the ridge towards Lose Hill passing Hollins Cross and Back Tor; return to Castleton via the public right of way that runs from Lose Hill

7 m

The Hope Valley

Farm via Riding House Farm and skirts the western side of Losehill Hall. Several old packhorse routes, now footpaths, meet at Hollins Cross. Indeed, it used to be the main road between Castleton and Edale and stories are still recalled of mill girls working in Edale who used to live in Castleton and walked this way to work, often having to spend the night at the mill when inclement weather prevented their return in the winter.

Losehill Hall is now a residential centre run by the Peak Park Joint Planning Board. From here are organised weekly courses covering many aspects of activities in the Peak District. Whether your interest is history, botany, geology, the history of old mines, caves, railways, or industrial archaeology of the area, all these interests and many more are catered for here.

A look on the map at the ground south of Rushop Edge shows various small streams which flow off the edge and suddenly disappear. These streams flow into a complex of underground passages which include Giants Hole and the very wet cave well known in caving circles as P8. Giants Hole lives up to its name for it is almost 500ft deep and a large system of passages leads out from its base. Just to the south of Giants Hole is Eldon Hole which is almost 200ft deep. Needless to say there are many other smaller cave systems and this particular area is very popular with cavers. Unfortnately many of the caves are watercourses and occasional cave rescue operations have to be mounted here.

Edale is not a very big village but it attracts thousands of visitors both during the summer months and in the winter when it is popular with skiers. It also marks the beginning of the Pennine Way and many ramblers can be seen climbing the path up Grindsbrook. This is a delightful path with many interesting views back towards the village and over to Hollins Cross and Back Tor. The path leads up onto Kinder Scout and it is

The Edale Valley

amazing just how many people head for this area ill prepared; for example, women in high heeled shoes and other people with inadequate footwear, without waterproof clothing etc. It needs to be clearly understood that Kinder Scout, Bleaklow and Saddleworth Moor beyond should not be treated lightly even in the summer. To put it bluntly, even in the summer these moors can be killers. This is not a case of trying to be melodramatic but simply stating facts. What can be a sunny pleasant day down in the valleys can turn into a nightmare with the descent of thick fog and mist up on the open moors and peat hags. Nonetheless for a well-prepared rambler they offer wide open spaces with freedom of movement virtually throughout the year. The only real problem to movement are the peat hags which give the impression of walking on a mattress and continually climbing up over the top of a peat hag, only drop down sometimes as much as ten feet to a little stream and then climb up to the top of the

next hag, before dropping to the next stream, and so on. It is not without good reason that Edale has a mountain rescue post and information centre. There are also three National Trust Information Barns in the Edale Valley.

Kinder Scout and Bleaklow

For those wishing to see the northern moors in a less strenuous manner there are two roads which cut through the moors. The northern one is the A628, the Woodhead road which heads towards Crowden from the Flouch Inn. On the western side of the watershed the valley becomes a long series of reservoirs built for Manchester Corporation. At the top is the oldest, Woodhead, followed by Torside, Rhodeswood, Valehouse and lastly Bottoms reservoir, almost on the outskirts of Tintwistle village. The more southerly route is the A57 road from Glossop to Sheffield. It is more commonly known as the Snake Road and both this and the Woodhead road feature regularly

Edale Village

Edale Church with Kinder Scout behind

in winter road bulletins as the announcer advises listeners that the roads are blocked by snow. Part of this road is the old Roman road from Brough to Glossop, and as earlier indicated in this chapter, parts of the old road can be seen on Doctor's Gate just to the north of this road, on Coldharbour Moor. Today's traveller can however obtain better comfort than his predecessors because the Duke of Devonshire built an inn, now known as the Snake Inn, in Ladyclough. If you do feel like doing a short walk without experiencing the rigours of the open moors why not take the footpath up Alport Dale to have a look at Alport Castles. This is not some medieval fortication but a natural outcrop in front of which is a large isolated mass of rock which became separated from the outcrop as a result of a landslip. Alport Castles are situated to the east of Alport Castles Farm which is about a mile up the dale from the main road at Alport Bridge.

To the west of the moors lie the small towns of Glossop and Hayfield which are joined by the A624. To the west of this road rises Coombes Edge, which marks the western boundary of the Peak District at this point. The boundary of the Peak Park skirts around the towns of Hayfield and Glossop, which developed as textile towns in the nineteenth century. Glossop is the larger of the two and has some interesting old buildings particularly around the town centre and in old Glossop to the east of the town. Hayfield however is a useful starting point for walking up on to the western edge of Kinder Scout and in particular for a walk to Kinder Downfall. The Downfall is a waterfall where the river Kinder flows off the edge of Kinder Scout. It is particularly well known for blowing back with the force of the wind, and quite often it freezes up during the harshness of the winter months. South of Kinder Downfall is Edale Cross sitting on a medieval packhorse road from Hayfield via Jacobs Ladder to Edale. These old roads inspired J.B.H. Ward to campaign that because of their very existence they proved that rights

Places of Interest around the Dark Peak

Longdendale
Series of five reservoirs in the valley leading up to the Woodland Pass between Holme Moss and Bleaklow.

Snake Pass
The A57 road between Glossop and Ladybower reservoir. Climbs over a gap between Bleaklow and Kinder Scout. The Snake Inn is situated near the top of the pass. Part of a paved Roman road ('Doctor's Gate') visible on Coldharbour Moor. Road and inn are named from the crest of the Cavendish family (Dukes of Devonshire), not from the road's twisting route.

Alport Dale
Delightful dale situated on the A57 just beyond the end of the Ashopton arm of the Ladybower reservoir. Gives access to Alport Castles.

Dinting Railway Centre
Steam railway centre near Glossop. Some large main line engines in steam may be seen.

Robin Hood's Picking Rods (Maiden Stones) Ludworth Moor, Glossop.
Two curious stones, possibly boundary stones or wayside crosses, set into the same base. One, unlikely, suggestion is that they were for bending bows while stringing them. Nearby is Monk's Road and Abbot's Chair (a cross base) and Basingwerk Abbey in Flintshire once owned land here.

Hayfield
Centre for discovering the western edge of Kinder Scout, including Kinder Downfall, the medieval packhorse road via Edale Cross and the upland area around Chinley Churn to the north-west.

Sett Trail, Hayfield
Walkway on the former railway line from Hayfield Station towards New Mills.

Bradfield and Low Bradfield
Two interesting villages set in Bradfield Dale to the east of the Strines Inn. The Dale Dyke Reservoir Dam collapsed in 1864. It destroyed much of Low Bradfield and settlements down the valley. A total of 238 people died, 700 animals drowned, more than 600 buildings were destroyed or damaged and 15 bridges were swept away. It was Britain's greatest dam disaster.

---

of way existed over the moors contrary to the wishes of the landowners. It was from Hayfield that a mass trepass took place in 1932, when several hundred people left the village to climb up on to Kinder. Despite the fact that the leaders were jailed after a show trial in Derby (one might even go so far as to say a staged trial) this was only the beginning. It was followed by other mass trespasses, political intrigue, double dealing and eventually the 1949 Act which paved the way for the open access agreements which now exist.

The Peak District National Park was founded as a result of the *National Parks and Access to the Countryside Act* of 1949, which gave the Peak Park Planning Board the authority to negotiate access agreements with local landowners to permit access to the open moorland, irrespective of whether rights of way across the land exist or not. The history of the fight for access has recently been documented by the late Howard Hill in his *Freedom to Roam* which deals with the struggles for access throughout Britain.

Access to the moors only exists where a right of way crosses the boundary of land classified as open land. The 'Dark Peak' OS Map shows the boundary of open land and the points of access. The beauty of the moors is that one can wander freely, but this does bring extra responsibility. Part of this is to respect the fact that on certain days in the shooting season, between 12 August and 10 December, parts of the moors are closed for grouse shooting. Notices are placed in villages, on railway stations and at access points around the moors giving details, or they are available from the Planning Board at Aldern House, Bakewell. Over £200,000 was raised by public subscription in the eighteen month leading up to June 1984, enabling the National Trust to acquire and

Grindsbrook

Sir Richard Arkwright's Masson Mill

Lea, Rhododendron Gardens

Back Tor from Nether Booth

Bradfield stocks

protect Kinder Scout.

Walks in the Area

In view of the fact that one can exercise one's own preference on the moors, certain routes are suggested in brief outline. These are perhaps the more interesting on the routes which cross the moors. It must be stressed again that the moors should not be crossed without adequate clothing, boots, food and with a compass and map. It is also useful to advise someone of your plans before setting out.

Hayfield, Kinder Downfall, Edale Cross
From Hayfield, take the road to Kinder Reservoir and then take the path up the northern side of Kinder Reservoir along White Brow. Proceed up William Clough until a convenient place to cross the brook is found and traverse the rising ground to Kinder Downfall. This can be a trying walk which can be avoided by taking the longer route to the cairn at the head of William Clough and walking down the edge of Kinder Scout along the Pennine Way to Kinder Downfall. Return via Edale Cross and Tunstead Clough Farm.

Edale, Grindsbrook Clough
Park in Edale village and walk up the road towards Grindsbrook and Kinder Scout. Cross the brook on the logbridge and walk up the valley eventually leaving the pasture. Eventually Edale Valley disappears from view and the path hugs the brook up onto the Kinder plateau. Follow the Pennine Way to Kinder Downfall. Return via Edale Cross and Jacob's Ladder to Upper Booth and then across the fields to Edale. The views from Upper Grindsbrook and on the descent from Jacob's Ladder are particularly memorable.

Alport Bridge, Howden Reservoir, Hagg Farm Youth Hostel
From Alport Bridge, just upstream from Hagg Farm Youth Hostel, owned and

operated by the Peak Park Planning Board, take the path that follows the track up to Alport Farm. Skirt the farm buildings and cross the brook before climbing up onto Birchinlee Pasture. The path follows Alport Castles Edge giving good views down Alport Dale and over to Kinder Scout. Take the path across Birchinlee Pasture and drop down the ridge above Ditch Clough into the wood. Walk along the road around to Howden Dam and on to Ouzelden Clough. From here a path climbs up out of the wood. It then follows the top of Gores Plantation, heading for Lockerbrook Farm, and Hagg Farm. Alport Bridge lies 1½ miles up the road.

There is a network of youth hostels which enable the northen moors to be crossed with the knowledge that a bed (booked in advance) is ahead. The walks described below, viz: Crowden to Edale or Hagg Farm; Hagg Farm to Langsett; and Langsett to Crowden are outlined as individual daily walks although it is possible to do the round trip of Crowden-Hagg Farm-Langsett-Crowden in a day. It is not recommended unless you are an experienced walker, however.

Crowden to Edale
From the hostel, walk around to the dam of Woodhead Reservoir and walk down the B6015 to almost opposite the hostel. Walk under the bridge carrying the railway and strike up the hill between Rollick Stones and Fair Vage Clough. Work around to Wildboarclough and follow this up to the top and on to Shining Clough Moss. Make for Far Moss and the Wain Stones on Bleaklow Head. From here, take the Pennine Way and follow this via Alport Low, across the Snake road and over Fetherbed Moss to Mill Hill. Here the route turns south-east heading for Kinder Downfall. Cross Kinder Scout and Edale Moor before dropping down Grindsbrook into Edale.

The route described above from the B6015 to Shining Clough Moss is not

16m

Windworn stones on Edale Moor

recommended other than for very fit walkers. An easier route is to walk around the reservoir from Crowden Youth Hostel via Torside dam and follow the Pennine Way up Clough Edge via Torside Castle to Bleaklow Head.

Crowden to Hagg Farm

11m Follow the route outlined above to the Wain Stones. From here a choice of routes are available. In either case, head for Grains in the Water. The more direct route follows the nearside of the River Alport above Alport Dale heading for Alport Castles. Proceed to Rowlee Pasture, finally leaving the access land near Bellhagg Farm, where a path passes the latter before dropping down to Hagg Farm.

12m The alternative route from Grains in the Water follows the ridge between Alport Dale and Upper North Grain,

heading for Oyster Clough. Follow the brook down the Clough until the Roman road is reached. Turn eastwards down this ancient, but narrow highway to Alport Bridge, which is just over a mile up the road from Hagg Farm. The former route is perhaps the best, affording much better views into the lower lying Alport Dale.

Hagg Farm to Langsett

2¹⁄ If one is actually heading for Langsett from Edale via Hagg Farm, a path skirting Kinder Scout runs from Clough Farm to Jaggers Clough, through the wood above the ruined Elim Pits Farm to Haggwater Bridge and on to Hagg Farm. From Hagg Farm take the path via Lockerbrook Farm to Derwent Reservoir. Follow the road that follows the valley up past Derwent village and Howden reservoirs to Slippery Stones,

12¹

where the Derwent village packhorse bridge was re-erected. Cross the bridge and take the path up Cut Gate on to Howden Edge. The path cuts across the moor to Mickleden Beck, dropping down towards Langsett. Cross Hingcliff Common to Brook House Bridge, climb the hill from the bridge to the top of the rise and turn right on the path through the woods to come into Langsett opposite the hostel.

Langsett to Crowden

Take the path opposite the hostel drive heading into the wood and taking the path to Swinden Farm. Take the track from the farm known as Swinden Lane and head west before turning to the A628 and Milton Lodge. Walk along the road, again westwards to the Dog & Partridge Inn. Just beyond here take the old road which bears off to the right and eventually crosses the main road at Cabin Hill and heads for Lady Cross and Salters Brook. The latter is a reminder of the old days when packhorses loaded with salt passed this way heading for Sheffield. The old track crosses the main road once more and the defined track maintains its height above the River Etherow and the main road. Eventually Woodhead reservoir is reached and the path drops down to the bridge over the spur of the reservoir. Follow the road for the last mile or so down to Crowden Youth Hostel. The hostel is open for non-members of the YHA.

Further Information

Telephone numbers are given where available. Opening times change of course and it is advisable to check beforehand to avoid disappointment. During the compilation of this gazetteer, recent information was used and then checked again at source. Consequently, this gazetteer represents the up to date position as at August 1984.

PLACES TO VISIT

Alton Towers
Alton, Stoke-on-Trent, Staffs
Tel: 0538 702200
Open: Easter-October, daily, grounds 9am-dusk; attractions 10am-5pm, 6pm or 7pm.
Alton Towers, Britain's only world-rated leisure park offers visitors a feast of fun, fantasy and excitement. More than seventy superb rides and shows are themed into one of the most magnificent settings in England — the former home of the Earls of Shrewsbury.

Bakewell Folk Museum
The Old House, Cunningham Place
Tel: Bakewell 3647
Open: April-October, daily, 2.30-5pm. Parties booked for morning or evening visits.

Buxton Micrarium
The Crescent, Buxton
Tel: Buxton 78662
Open: March-October, daily.
Exhibition of nature beneath the microscope.

Buxton Museum and Art Gallery
Terrace Road
Tel: Buxton 4658
Open: daily except Sunday.
Antiquities and geological specimens, art exhibitions.

Chatterley Whitfield Mining Museum
Tunstall
Stoke on Trent
Tel: (0782) 813337
Open: daily (except Saturday, October-February)
Ride the cage 700ft below ground. See and hear the 'living story' of coal as told by guides with a lifetimes mining experience.

Chatsworth Estate Farm Shop
Pilsley
Open: Monday-Saturday, 9am-5.30pm.
Produce from the estate is on sale including game when in season.

Chatworth House
Bakewell
Tel: Baslow 2204
Open: March-October, (dates may vary a little), daily, 11.30am-4.30pm.
Farming and forestry exhibition and adventure playground; open end March-end September, 10.30am-5.30pm.
There is a family admission to the farmyard and adventure playground. For the price of two adults and one child, up to three more children go in free. No dogs (but dog pound provided).

Dinting Railway Centre
Glossop 5596
Open: all year. Steam days on most
summer Sundays and Bank Holidays.

Eyam Museum (Private)
Tel: Hope Valley 31010
Admission by appointment.
Curator: Clarence Daniel.

Foxfield Light Railway
Dilhorne, Cheadle, Staffs
Open: April-September, Sunday and
Bank Holiday at former colliery.
Steam trains on three miles of private
line. Also static display of locomotives.
Details from Mr A Green,
94 Wellington Road, Bollington,
Macclesfield, Cheshire
Tel: Macclesfield (0625) 73567

Gawsworth Hall
Gawsworth, Maccesfield
Tel: North Rode 456
Open: April-October, daily, 2-6pm.
Fifteenth-century manor house, between
Macclesfield and Congleton.

Gulliver's Kingdom
Temple Walk, Matlock Bath
Tel: Matlock 55970
Open: Easter-September, daily, 1-6pm.
Closed Friday except in high season.
Turn up the hill to the south of and
opposite the Pavilion.
Party rates available. Staff help available
for wheelchairs on the slopes.
Model Village and Children's Fantasy
Land.

Haddon Hall
Bakewell
Tel: Bakewell 2855
Open: Tuesday-Saturday
Magnificent medieval house.

High Tor
Matlock
Access from near Matlock Bath Station,
Church Street or Dale Road, Matlock or
from Starkholmes.
Open: daily, 10am-dusk.
60 acres of grounds, walks and extensive
views.

Lea Rhododendron Gardens
Lea, Matlock
Tel: Dethick 380
Open: Easter-end July, daily.

Lyme Hall and Park (National Trust)
Disley, Stockport, Cheshire
Tel: Disley 2023
Open: Hall, March-October; Park all
year round.
The largest stately home in Cheshire,
with many fine treasures.

Matlock Bath Aquarium
North Parade, Matlock Bath
Tel: Matlock 3624
Open: daily in summer and weekends in
winter, 11am-5.30pm.

Midland Railway Steam Centre
Butterley, Nr Ripley, Derbys
Collection of railwayana, locomotives
and rolling stock dedicated to the
Midland Railway.

**North Staffordshire Steam Railway
Centre**
Cheddleton Station, Cheddleton, Leek,
Staffs
Tel: Churnet Side 360522
Open: June-September, daily (except
Saturday), 11am-4pm; Sundays and
Bank Holidays; the rest of the year
11am-dusk.
Working steam (Sundays only) railway
museum of the North Staffordshire
Railway, offering 12 mile 'Churnetrail'
Scenic Cruise Trains through the

magnificent Churnet Valley. Every
Sunday June-September (inclusive) plus
all Bank Holidays.

Ollerenshaw Collection
(The Cavendish House Museum)
Cross Street, Castleton
Tel: Hope Valley 20642
Open: daily, 9.30am-6pm (dusk in
winter).
Adjoining the Blue John Stone Craft
Shop. Private museum of Derbyshire
treasures, including one of the largest
and finest collections of Blue John
Stone.

Peveril Castle
Castleton
Open: daily, expect over Christmas.
Norman Castle founded in 1068. In care
of Department of Environment.

Riber Castle Wildlife Park
Matlock
Tel: Matlock 2073
Open: 10am-6pm (closes earlier in
winter).
Discount for parties of 20 or more.

Silk Museum
Paradise Mill, Old Park Lane,
Macclesfield.
Tel: 0625 618228
Open: Tuesday-Sunday, 2-5pm.
Display of silk looms. Guided tours
available with demonstrations. Shop.
Tea-room in nearby Heritage Centre.

Sudbury Hall (National Trust)
Sudbury, Derbys DE6 5HT
Tel: Sudbury (028 378) 305
Open: April-October, Wednesday-
Sunday plus Bank Holiday Mondays, 1-
5.30pm.
Charles II house with fine late
seventeenth-century decoration, plus
Museum of Childhood.

The National Tramway Museum
Crich
Tel: Ambergate 2565
Open: April-October, weekends and
Bank Holidays, 10.30am-6.30pm; May-
September, Monday-Thursday, 10am-
5.30pm.
Collection of trams from home and
overseas. Unlimited rides on $1\frac{1}{2}$ miles of
tram tracks.

NATURE RESERVES AND TRAILS

Coombs Valley Nature Reserve
Six Oaks Farm, Nr Apesford, Leek,
Staffs
Open: Tuesday, Thursday and
weekends.

Hawksmoor Nature Reserve
Near Cheadle
Situated at Greendale on Oakamoor-
Cheadle road. There are three trails
here.

Ilam Nature Trail
A $1\frac{1}{2}$ mile trail in grounds of Ilam Hall.
Details from National Trust shop
adjacent to the hall and car park.

Errwood Hall Trail
Goyt Valley
Forestry Commission trail around the
old hall's estate.

Black Rocks Trail
Bolehill, near Wirksworth
Three Forestry Commission trails of 1,
$1\frac{1}{2}$ and 2 miles length.

Sett Valley Trail
Former railway line from Hayfield
Station.

Tissington Trail
Former railway line from Parsley Hay to
Ashbourne.

High Peak Trail
Former railway line from High Peak Junction (Cromford Canal) south of Cromford to Hurdlow.

Monsal Trail
Former railway line from Chee Dale to Rowsley.

Staffordshire Way
Long distance path from Bosley Cloud southwards through the county. Full details from Leek information centre.

The Royston Grange Trail
Britain's first archaeological trail, some four miles in length. Situated between Youlgreave and Ashbourne. Guide book available from Peak Park Planning Board Information Centres or Aldern House, Baslow Road, Bakewell.

Deep Hayes Country Park
Situated at Wallgrange, which is on the road to Cheddleton from Longsdon, south-west of Leek.
Waymarked nature trail and Information Centre. Site of former reservoir reduced in size when doubts arose about the stability of the dam. Now three smaller pools. Caldon Canal adjoins the Park.
Visitor Centre open: May-September, Saturday and Sunday, 2-5pm.

Discovery Trails
The Peak Park Joint Planning Board organises 'Discovery Trails' led by experienced people and designed for individuals and families rather than organised groups. Prior booking, by telephone only, is essential. The subjects covered are numerous and well recommended. A small fee is charged. Details from National Park Office, tel: Bakewell 4321.

Walks with a Warden
The National Trust also provides a series of 'Walks with a Warden' throughout the Peak District. Again, booking by telephone is essential. Details from the East Midlands Regional Office, tel: Worksop 486411.

SHOW CAVES

Blue John Cavern
Mam Tor, Castleton
Tel: Hope Valley 20638
Open: daily, 9.30am-6pm, winter 9.30am-4pm.
Old mine workings for Blue John stone. The largest range of caverns containing veins of the stone.

Treak Cliff Cavern
Castleton
Tel: Hope Valley 20571
Open: daily, 9.30am-6pm, winter 9.30am-4pm.

Speedwell Cavern
Winnats Pass, Castlton
Tel: Hope Valley 20512
Open: daily, 10am-6pm throughout the year.
Visitors travel by boat along flooded mine level to natural cavern.

Pooles Cavern
Green Lane, Buxton
Tel: Buxton 6978
Open: Easter-November, daily, closed Wednesday (except high season) 10am-5pm.
Facilities include 100-acre country park, exhibition and picnic area.

Bagshawe Cavern
Bradwell, Near Castleton
Tel: Hope Valley 20540
Open: March-October, Saturday-Thursday 2-6pm; November-February by appointment only.
In addition to the show cave, there is an adventure trip, by appointment only.

Temple Mine
Matlock Bath
Details of this new venture may be
obtained from the Peak District Mining
Museum at Matlock Bath.
Tel: Matlock 3834

Peak Cavern
Castleton
Tel: Hope Valley 20285
Open: Easter-mid-September, daily,
10am-5pm.

Heights of Abraham
Matlock Bath
Tel: Matlock 2365
Open: Easter-end September, daily,
10am-6pm (later in high season). Great
Masson Cavern: Sunday and Bank
holiday weekends, 10am-6pm. Also
open in midweek in high season (ring for
details).
Turn up Holme Road opposite the
railway station or use the cable car
which starts on the up river side of the
railway station. Two show caves, Tree
Tops visitor centre and the Victoria
prospect tower.

The Royal Cave
Matlock Bath
Tel: Matlock 55970 or 3654
Adjacent to Gulliver's Kingdom.
Open: Easter-end September, 11am-
4.30pm. Closed Friday except in high
season. Party rates available.

ARCHAEOLOGICAL SITES

Arbor Low Stone Circle
Large stone circle two miles south of
Monyash in the care of the Department
of the Environment.

Bridestones Chambered Tomb
Large standing stones situated close to
the minor road between Congleton and
Rushton, Staffs, south of Bosley Cloud.

Croxden Abbey
Great Gates, nr Rocester, Staffs
Former Cistercian Abbey with
substantial remains; in the care of the
Department of the Environment.

Peveril Castle,
Castleton
Stone keep and outer wall, in the care of
the Department of the Environment.
Situated on the hill overlooking the
village.

Five Wells Chambered Tomb
Situated north-west of Chelmorton. It is
not on a footpath but may be seen from
the A6 by the Waterloo Hotel near
Taddington.

Nine Ladies Stone Circle
Stanton Moor
Situated north-west of Birchover.
Remains of a bell barrow with the earth
mound removed. The remains of some
seventy barrows have been investigated
on Stanton Moor.

Nine Stones Circle,
Harthill Moor
North of Robin Hood's Stride, not on,
but visible from a public footpath. Only
four very large standing stones remain.

Hermit's Cave,
Cratcliffe Rocks
Situated to the east of Robin Hood's
Stride, 1½ miles due west of Birchover.
Contains a crucifix carved at the back of
the cave.

Carl Wark Iron Age Fort,
nr Longshaw
Iron Age fort situated adjacent to the
path from the top of Padley Gorge
towards Stanage Edge.

Mam Tor Iron Age Fort,
nr Castleton
Prominently sited on the top of Mam
Tor, north-west of Castleton Village.

The Peakland Archaeological Society
undertakes field work in the Peak
District and many of their finds are
displayed in Buxton Museum. The
Bateman collection of cinerary urns and
skulls, together with the Heathcote
Collection of artifacts from Stanton
Moor, are housed in Sheffield Museum.

INDUSTRIAL ARCHAEOLOGY

Middleton Top Winding Engine House
Tel: Wirksworth 3204
Open: Sundays. Engine also operates on
first Saturday of each month.
Approach from Middleton-by-
Wirksworth by side of Rising Sun pub.
Look for tall chimney on hill above
village.

Arkwright's Cromford Mill
Mill Lane, Cromford
Tel: Wirksworth 4297
Open: Wednesday-Sunday inclusive,
evening and guided tours by
arrangement.
Small exhibition and audio visual
display. The Arkwright Society acquired
the mill site in 1979. Since then work has
been undertaken with the aim of clearing
the site of modern industrial use to
reveal the fabric of the world's first
successful water-powered cotton
spinning mill.

Mandale Mine
Lathkilldale, SK196662
Remains of Cornish-type engine house,
waterwheel pit, sough entrance and
aqueduct piers.

Caudwell's Mill
Rowsley
Tel: Matlock 734374
Historic water powered flour mill.
Guided tours day or evening, weekends
included. Special open days throughout
the season. Flour on sale throughout the
year.

Lea Wood Pumping Station
Cromford
Tel: Wirksworth 3727
Fifty inch, Cornish-type beam engine,
fully restored and steamed periodically.
Enquiries to Cromford Canal Society
Ltd, Old Wharf, Mill Lane, Cromford,
Matlock, Derbys.

Stone Edge Chimney
Near B5057 Darley Dale to Chesterfield
Road. SK334669.
The oldest free standing industrial
chimney in Britain built around 1770.
Remains of old lead mining cupola at its
base, including several flues and small
reservoir to power bellows for a small
blast furnace.

Magpie Mine
Sheldon SK173682
Mining remains visible from the road.
The Peak District Mining Museum run
guided tours on occasions around the
site. The remains include a Cornish-type
engine house with chimneys, remains of
a steam whim, more recent head gear
last used in 1958 and a replica horse
whim.

Peak District Lead Mining Museum
The Pavilion, Matlock Bath
Tel: Matlock 3834
Central exhibit is a huge water pressure
engine built in 1819 and recovered from
a lead mine at Winster. Displays of
geology, minerals and mining in the
Peak from Roman times.

Masson Mill
Cromford, SK294573
View from road only. Erected by
Arkwright in 1783. The original six-
storey mill is at the north end of the site.

Holme Mine
Bakewell, SK214693 (approx)
Old chert mine being developed for
tourists. Check details at Peak District
Mining Museum, Matlock Bath.

Monsal Dale Viaduct
SK183715
Old railway viaduct on the former
Midland Railway.

Hartington Signal Box
SK149610
A remnant of the old London and North
Western Railway's line between Buxton
and Ashbourne. Converted to an
information centre. Contains old lever
frames etc and several photographs of
the old railway.

Hulme End Station
SK104594
Former railway buildings of the Leek
and Manifold Valley Light Railway.
Surviving are the booking office and
engine shed.

Cressbrook Mill
Monsal Dale, SK173728
Built in 1815 to replace Arkwright's
smaller mill which had been built in
1779. Premises now incorporate a
squash club.

Bugsworth Basin
SK020822
Large canal basins and wharfs of the
Peak Forest Canal including track bed
of horse drawn tram roads, lime kilns
etc.

Marple Bridge
SJ961885
Imposing set of stair locks on the Peak
Forest Canal. Warehouse supposedly
built by Arkwright in 1794-1800. Large
aquaduct some 80ft high carrying the
canal over the river Goyt with three 60ft
spans.

Calver Mill
SK245744
A seven-storey cotton mill of 1803. Not
open to the public, exterior only.

Bamford Mill
SK205834
Cotton mill built about 1792 retaining
its 30ft x 22ft wide waterwheel and a
1907 tandem-compound steam engine.
The present owners have open days each
year when the engine is run under
stream. They also admit visitors at other
times by prior appointment. Details
available from Carbolite Furnaces Ltd,
Bamford Mill, Bamford, Sheffield S30
2AU. Tel: Hope Valley 51551.

Cromford Canal
High Peak Wharf, SK313560
Many old buildings survive at the
junction of the Cromford and High Peak
Railway and the Cromford Canal. The
majority of these are situated at the foot
of Sheep Pasture Incline and the large
wheel around which the cable ran still
survives. Nearby on the canal is an
aqueduct over the river Derwent and the
Lea Wood Pumphouse (see separate
entry). Visitor Centre recently opened.

Caldon Canal
Froghall, SK027478
Various old canal wharf buildings
together with the bottom section of the
incline to Cauldon Lowe Limestone
Quarries. Adjacent to the wharf is a
large bank of lime kilns now preserved.

Caldon Canal
Hazelhurst Locks, Denford
SJ948538
The junction of the Caldon Canal with
its Leek branch. There is a flight of
locks, aqueduct and attractive cast iron
bridge.

Brindley Mill
Mill Street, Leek, Staffs
Tel: Leek 384195 & 381446
Open: Easter-October, Weekend and
Bank Holiday Mondays, 2-5pm; July
and August, Monday, Tuesday and
Thursday.
Water powered cornmill with museum
devoted to James Brindley.

Good Luck Mine
Via Gellia, SK270565
A typical small lead mine now opened to
visitors on the first Sunday in every
month.

PICNIC PLACES

W/C indicates toilet facilities available
W/C-d indicates toilet facilities for the
disabled also available

Waterhouses: SK085502 W/C-d
Lamaload Reservoir: SK975753 W/C
Errwood Reservoir, Goyt Valley:
SK012748 and SK012731. A toilet
(W/C-d) has been built at the eastern
end of Errwood Dam.
Tittesworth Reservoir, Meerbrook:
SJ994603 W/C Children's play area.
Calton Lees, near Chatsworth:
SK258685 W/C
Derbyshire Bridge, Goyt Valley:
SK017718 W/C-d
Goyts Clough Quarry, Goyt Valley:
SK012735 W/C
Teggs Nose, Nr Macclesfield Forest:
SJ950733 W/C Information Centre
Tideswell Dale: SK154742 W/C

Moor Lane, Youlgreave: SK194645
White Lodge, Monsal Dale:
SK171706 W/C
Froghall Canal Wharf: SK027478
Also canalside restaurant W/C
Oakamoor, site of Bolton's Works:
SK053448 W/C
Ilam Hall: SK132507 W/C-d (females
only). Information Centre, Café.
Tissington Trail:
Mapleton Lane: SK175469 Water for
horses
Thorpe: SK165503 Shelter (no picnic
tables)
Tissington: SK177521 W/C-d
Alsop-en-de-Dale: SK156549
Shelter
Hartington: SK150611 W/C
Information Centre
Parsley Hay: SK147636 W/C-d
Hurdlow: SK127659
High Peak Trail:
Friden: SK173607
Mininglow: SK195582
Middleton Top Engine House:
SK276552 W/C
Black Rocks: SK291557 W/C
High Peak Junction: SK313560
W/C
Edale: SK124853 W/C-d
Mam Nick, Rushop Edge: SK124833
Stanage, Hollin Bank: SK237838 W/C-d
Blore Pasture (overlooks Dovedale):
SK136498 W/C
Cromford Meadows: SK300571
Butterley Hill, Tansley Moor: SK349598
W/C
Darley Dale: SK270624
Matlock Moor: SK324633
Lyme Hall: SJ963825 W/C (National
Trust)
Derwent Reservoir: SK173893
Fairholmes Cycle Hire Centre W/C-d
Over Haddon: SK204664 W/C-d
Hayfield (former station) on Sett Valley
Trail: SK035869 W/C-d
Longshaw Lodge: SK266802 W/C-d.

Information Centre (National Trust), café.

The above Picnic Areas all have tables and seats. The places mentioned below do not, but off-the-road car parking is available.

Ashford-in-the-Water: SK215768 W/C-d
Adjoining Matlock Bath Railway Station: SK298584 W/C
Matlock Dale (near High Tor): SK297595 W/C Fishing
Baslow: SK260720 W/C
Baslow Edge: SK261748
Rudyard Lake: SJ951583 W/C Public Slipway
Weags Bridge, Manifold Valley: SK100542
Wetton Mill, Manifold Valley: SK096561 Café W/C
Alstonfield: SK131556 W/C
Hulme End: SK104594 (NB OS White Peak map symbol is in the wrong place)
Longnor Village: SK089649 W/C
Cisterns Clough, Axe Edge: SK034698
Thorpe Village: SK156505 W/C-d
Castleton: SK149829 W/C-d
Hathersage: SK232814 W/C
Hope: SK170835 W/C
Wetton: SK109553 W/C-d
Elton Common: SK226598
Monsal Head: SK185715 W/C

GAME FISHING

Certain hotels have fishing rights available to guests. These include:

Bamford: Marquis of Granby Hotel,
 Tel: Hope Valley 51206

Baslow: Cavendish Hotel,
 Tel: Baslow 2311
 River Wye: Three rods, Cressbrook

Mill down to Ashford Marble works (approx 4½ miles)
River Derwent: Three rods, Calver Bridge, east side, and St Mary's Wood, west side, down to Smelting Mill Brook

Rowsley (6½ miles) Brown trout are restocked annually from Chatsworth's ponds and rainbow trout and grayling breed naturally.

Hartington: Charles Cotton Hotel,
 Tel: Hartington 229
 300 yards of the River Dove

Ilam: Izaak Walton Hotel,
 Tel: Thorpe Cloud 261

Longnor: Crewe & Harpur Arms Hotel,
 Tel: Longnor 205
 Seven miles of trout fishing — wet or dry,
 eight rods issued daily.

Rowsley: Peacock Hotel,
 Tel: Darley Dale 3518
 Trout, seven miles of River Wye;
 Grayling, two miles of river Derwent.

Rowsley: Grouse & Claret,
 Tel: Darley Dale 3233
 Matlock Bath: New Bath Hotel,
 Tel: Matlock 3275

Matlock: The Midland Hotel,
 Tel: Matlock 2630
 River Derwent from Hall Leys Park Matlock to Cromford.

The Peak Park Joint Planning Board issues a leaflet on fishing in its *Fact Finder* series of leaflets.

RESERVOIR FISHING

For permission to fish the area's reservoirs contact the appropriate water authority.

Lady Bower
Derwent
Severn Trent Water Authority (Derwent Division), Dimple Road, Matlock, Derbys.

Tittesworth (also bird watching)
Severn Trent Water Authority (Upper Trent Division), Westport Road, Burslem, Stoke-on-Trent, Staffs.

Dam Flask
Dunford Bridge
Yorkshire Water Authority, West Riding House, 67 Albion Street, Leeds 1.

Errwood
Valehouse
Bottoms
Lamaload
Ridgegate
Teggsnose
North West Water Authority, Rivers Division, New Town House, Buttermarket Street, Warrington, Cheshire.

Rudyard Lake
British Waterways Board, Reservoir Attendant, Reservoir Cottage, Rudyard Lake, Leek, Staffs.

Dam Flask Reservoir
Sheffield Viking Sailing Club,
Mr A.J. Pemberton, 41 Chelsea Road, Sheffield 11.

Bottoms Lodge Reservoir
Glossop and District Sailing Club,
Mrs R. Mason, 23 Edale Close, Hazelgrove, Stockport, Cheshire.

Dove Stones Reservoir
Dove Stones Sailing Club,
Mr J. Ball, 28 Dorset Avenue, High Crompton, Shaw, Lancs.

Rudyard Lake
Casual visitors should contact the Reservoir Attendant, Reservoir Cottage, Rudyard Lake, Leek, for details.

Tarside
Glossop Sailing Club,
Mrs R. Mason, 23 Edale Close, Hazelgrove, Stockport, Cheshire.

Combs
Details from North West Water Authority, Rivers Division, Buttermarket Street, Warrington, Cheshire.

Where sailing is allowed on reservoirs the relevant water authority has delegated responsibility for the sailing on that water to various clubs. In some cases these clubs allow the casual visitor and therefore it is necessary to write to the relevant club if you wish to use their water.

Errwood Reservoir
Errwood Sailing Club,
Mr A. Gay, Four Oaks, The Coppice, Higher Poynton, Cheshire.

The Derbyshire and Lancashire Gliding Club,
Camphill Farm, Great Hucklow, Buxton, Derbys.
Tel: Buxton 871270
Full details of membership, holiday courses etc are available from the steward. In addition to the clubhouse, facilities include overnight accommodation, a full catering service and childrens playground. The club currently owns eight gliders.

Staffordshire Gliding Club,
Morridge, Leek, Staffs.

This club operates at weekends only and has no resident steward. For further information contact B.H. Rowding, 22 High Storrs Close, Sheffield S11 7LT. Tel: Sheffield 668597. The club has no post box at the club site.

HANG GLIDING

Peak District Flight Training School, Macclesfield Road, Leek, Staffs.
Tel: Leek 383659 or Blackshaw 205
The oldest BHGA registered school. Hang gliders are also manufactured by the same firm. Accommodation arranged for you.

Peak School of Hang Gliding,
65c Berry Hedge Lane, Winshill,
Burton on Trent, Staffs.
Tel: 0283 43879
Two and four day courses based at Ilam Hall Youth Hostel. Accommodation available at the hall or nearby.

SWIMMING POOLS

There are pools at Leek, Cheadle, Ashbourne, Buxton, Glossop, Matlock and Chesterfield. plus an open air swimming pool at Hathersage with heated and filtered water, open May to mid-September (closed on Sundays).

SQUASH COURTS

There are squash courts at Ashbourne; Callow Park, Wirksworth; Leek; Glossop; Sheffield; and Cressbrook Mill, Monsal Dale.

CANAL CRUISES

Caldon Canal: Froghall Basin
Situated off the A52 on Foxt Road at Froghall
Tel: Ipstones 486
Regular $2\frac{1}{2}$-hour horse drawn trips on Thursday and Sunday at 2pm with additional trips on Bank Holidays. On the first and third Saturday in the summer months there is also a $3\frac{1}{2}$-hour trip including a four-course meal; also afternoon teas on the canal are very popular. Telephone in advance.

Peak Forest Canal
For weekly hired boats contact Coles Morton Marine Ltd, Canal Wharf, Whaley Bridge, Stockport, Cheshire
Tel: Whaley Bridge 2226

Caldon Canal: Cheddleton
A variety of different cruises are available during the summer months, taking $2\frac{1}{4}$ to 6 hours. Booking required to M.E. Braine, Norton Canes Docks, Lime Lane, Pelsall, Walsall, Staffs.
Tel: Brownhills (05433) 4888 or 0889 881328
These cruises offer an opportunity of seeing the beautiful Churnet Valley other than on foot.

Cromford Canal, Cromford
Enquiries to Cromford Canal Society Ltd, Old Wharf, Mill Lane, Cromford, Matlock, Derbys.
Tel: Wirksworth 3727
Forty-minutes horse drawn trip from Cromford Wharf. Currently Saturday, Sunday and Bank Holidays 2pm and 4pm plus passenger and charter trips midweek. Details subject to change, so telephone in advance.

GOLF

Buxton and High Peak Club,
Fairfield Common, Buxton — 18
holes
Cavendish Golf Club, Buxton
— 18 holes
Chapel-en-le-Frith — 18 holes
Bamford — 18 holes
New Mills — 9 holes
Glossop — 9 holes
Birchall Golf Club,
Cheddleton Road, Leek — 18 hole
Westwood Golf Club,
Newcastle Road, Leek — 9 holes
Whiston Golf Club.
Whiston, Stoke-on-Trent, Staffs
— 18 holes
Stockton Brook Golf Club,
Stockton Brook, Stoke-on-Trent
— 18 holes
Matlock Golf Club,
Chesterfield Road, Matlock, Derbys
— 18 holes
Clifton Golf Club,
Clifton, Ashbourne, Derbys — 9 holes
Bakewell Golf Club — 9 holes
Sheffield has eleven golf clubs including
three municipal clubs, viz: Beauchief,
Concord Park and Tinsley Park.

RIDING STABLES

Endon Riding School,
Coltslow Farm, Stanley Moss Lane,
Stockton Brook, near Stoke-on-Trent
Tel: Stoke-on-Trent 502114

Northfield Farm
Flash, near Buxton
Tel: Buxton 2543

Consall Valley Stables,
Consall Forge, Wetley Rocks
Tel: Stoke-on-Trent 550049

Curbar Edge School,
'Emberbrook' Bar Road, Curbar,
Calver, Sheffield S30 1YA
Tel: Hope Valley 30584

Red House Stables,
Old Road, Darley Dale, Matlock
Tel: Matlock 733583

Rushop Hall
Chapel-en-le-Frith
Tel: Chapel-en-le-Frith 3323

Hopkin Farm
Tansley, Matlock
Tel: Matlock 2253

Lady Booth
Edale
Tel: Hope Valley 70205

Spring Paddock School
Marple Road, Charlesworth,
Hyde
Tel: Glossop 3175

Moorlands Trailriding
Glenwood House Farm, Ipstones,
Staffs
Tel: Ipstones 762
Not a school or centre. Trailriding
holidays through the Peak District,
covering up to 25 miles a day.

CAVING

The many caves and mines should *never*
be entered by the inexperienced. Two
useful addresses are:

Derbyshire Caving Association,
c/o East Midlands Area Office, The
Sports Council, 26 Musters Road,
West Bridgeford, Nottingham.

Peak District Mines Historical Society,
Peak District Mining Museum,
Matlock Bath

**Cave Rescue: Dial 999 and ask for Cave
Rescue.**

CYCLE HIRE CENTRES

Tissington Trail, High Peak Trail. Bikes may be hired from both Ashbourne and Parsley Hay station sites. The latter is situated just north of the old Hartington Station. Also Middleton Top Engine House. There is usually no need to book except for parties. Open from March to October.

Lyme Park, Lyme Hall, Disley, Stockport, Cheshire.
Tel: Disley 2032
A useful way of exploring this 1,300-acre park.

A.J. & M. Sears
Market Place, Hartington, Buxton.
Tel: Hartington 459
Open: daily, except during January and February then weekends only.

Derwent Reservoir
Tel: Hope Valley 51261
Roughly two miles north of Ashopton viaduct.

Monsal Head Cycle Hire,
Monsal Head, Bakewell
Tel: Great Longstone 505 or Tideswell 871679
Open: April-September, daily, 9.30am-7pm; October-March, normally open every day except Christmas Day, but telephone in advance for midweek useage.

WELL DRESSING

May: Ashford, Etwall, Tissington, Wirksworth (Spring Bank Holiday)
June: Tideswell, Youlgreave
July: Bakewell, Hope, Pilsley, Stoney Middleton
August: Barlow, Bradwell, Endon, Wormhill

September: Hartington

Exact dates are available from tourist information centres.

SHOWS, DISPLAYS, ETC

Leek Agricultural Show
Bakewell Agricultural Show
Hope Show, August
Hartington Sports: (chiefly horse jumping), nearest Saturday to 20 September.
Flagg Races (High Peak Hunt Point to Point), Tuesday after Easter
Longnor Sports Day. Usually 1st or 2nd Thursday in September.
Matlock Bath Illuminations and Firework Display, with parade of illuminated boats. Details from Matlock Information Centre.
Cromford Steam Traction Rally, Cromford Meadows. 1st weekend in August.
Grand Transport Extravaganza, Crich Tramway Museum, August Bank Holiday.
Ashbourne Carnival, July.
Ashbourne Show, August
Glossop Carnival. First weekend in July.
Leek Club Day Procession (for Sunday Schools)
Leek Carnival
Manifold Valley Agricultural Show, First Saturday in August, held on Archford Moor, south of Hulme End, near Hartington.

FESTIVALS

Alport Castles Love Feast: 1st Sunday in July, 1.30pm. Further details from the Methodist Minister, The Manse, Hathersage, Sheffield,
Tel: Hope Valley 50305
Ashbourne Shrovetide Football: Shrove Tuesday and Ash Wednesday, 2pm.

Castleton Garlanding: 29 May
(except when on a Sunday)
Chatsworth House runs several festivals
and fairs. For full details Tel: Baslow
2204.
May: Angling Fair
June: Brass Band Festival
July (beginning): Show Jumping
September: Country Sport Spectacular
including over 150 trade stands
October: Horse Trials
Eyam Plague Service of Remembrance
at Cuckett Delf on last Sunday in
August at 3pm.
Jenkin Chapel Saltersford: 2nd Sunday
in September, Open Air Service 3pm.
Macclesfield Forest Chapel Rush
Bearing: Sunday nearest 12 August
3pm.
Garsworth Open Air Theatre Festival.
Held annually, for a month starting the
last week in June.
Padley Pilgrimage: Thursday nearest
12 July, 3pm at Grindleford Station
Taddington Steam Rally

The Peak Park Joint Planning Board
publishes a calendar of events each year
which is very useful.

CRAFT CENTRES

J. Peck & Son, Belmont Hall, Ipstones,
Leek, Staffs
Tel: Ipstones 391
High quality hand-made pine furniture
to order. Appointment necessary.

Old Shop Craft Pottery, High Street,
Alton, Staffs
Tel: Oakamoor 702065
Open: every afternoon and Monday,
Tuesday and Wednesday mornings.
Decorated earthenware, stoneware,
sculpture.

Staffordshire Peak Arts Centre,
The Old School, Cauldon Lowe,
Nr Waterhouses
Tel: Waterhouses 431

Brian Asquith, ARCA, FSIA,
Designer Craftsman, 'Turret House'
Youlgreave
Tel: Youlgreave (062 986) 204
Open: Monday to Friday,
10am-1pm and 2-4pm

Rookes Pottery,
Mill Lane, Hartington,
Buxton
Tel: Hartington 650
Terracotta Gardenware and Gifts.

Chapel House Turnery,
Tideswell.
Tel: Buxton 871096
Hand-made goods in English timber.

Derbyshire Craft Centre,
Calver Bridge, Near Baslow
Tel: Hope Valley (0433) 31231.
Craft Shop and Eating House
Open: 10am-6pm, 7 days a week.

Andrew Sharpe,
Baileys Mill, The Cliff,
Matlock
Tel: Matlock (0629) 55560.
Open: Monday to Saturday
8am-6pm week-days and
8am-12noon on Saturday.

Phillip Withers (Silver Workshops)
Saracen's Head Farm, Brailsford, on
A52 between Derby and Ashbourne.
Tel: Brailsford 730.
Open by appointment.

Fox Country Furniture,
Church Street, Longnor, Buxton.
Tel: Longnor 496
Furniture in elm and oak.

The Gallery,
4 West End, Wirksworth
Tel: Wirksworth 3557
Open: Tuesday, Thursday to Saturday
10.30am-5pm
Pottery and prints.

Andrew Lawton Furniture,
Goatscliffe, Grindleford, Sheffield.
Open: weekdays 10am-6pm; weekends
by arrangement.
Hand-made furniture

Cameron Pearson,
Coulsden Cottage, Bath Street,
Bakewell
Telephone: Bakewell 3919
Open: weekdays (except Tuesday am),
9am-5pm, also Saturday am.
Founders of letters and signs in cast
aluminium, brass and bronze.

Nigel Griffiths, Old cheese Factory,
Grange Mill, Near Winster
Telephone: Winster 720
Open: Monday-Saturday, 9am-5pm.
Hand-made furniture

Cargo Leathergoods,
North Street, Cromford
Tel: Wirksworth 4574
Open: daily (except Thursday),
10am-6pm, Sunday 2-6pm.
Leather accessories

The Coach House, Lea Green, near
Matlock
Tel: Dethick 346
Open: April-end December, daily,
12 noon-6pm.
Craftshop, farmhouse teas, ice cream
parlour.

Frank Pratt, Old Grammar School,
Church Walk, Wirksworth
Tel: Wirksworth 2828
Open: Monday-Friday, 9am-5pm,
Saturday, 9am-1pm. Saturday pm
and Sunday by prior arrangement
Hand-made furniture

Spencer Crafts,
The Riddings Farm, Kirk Ireton,
Ashbourne
Tel: Ashbourne 70331
Open: by appointment.
Furniture restoration and cabinet
making.

Fosters Sporting Services,
32 St John Street, Ashbourne
Tel: Ashbourne 43135
Open: am daily (except Wednesday and
Saturday 9am-5pm), 9am-5.30pm,
Closed Sunday.
Hand-built fishing rods and
equipment.

W.M. Haycock; North Leys,
Ashbourne.
Tel: Ashbourne 42395
Open: Monday-Friday, 9am-5pm,
other times by appointment.
Clock and regulator works. The last
survivor of Ashbournes' clock
industry.
Wall clocks, bracket and grandfather
clocks made on the premises.

Paul Eden Clocks.
Buxton Road, Longnor, Buxton,
Derbyshire.
Tel: Longnor 493
Open: Easter-September, Monday-
Saturday, 10am-6pm, Sunday, 2-5pm.
Winter by appointment.
Kitchen clocks, longcase clocks, etc,
some available in kit form.

PLACES OF INTEREST SURROUNDING THE
DISTRICT

Gladstone Pottery Museum
Uttoxeter Road, Longton, Stoke-on-
Trent
Tel: Stoke-on-Trent 319232
Open: Monday-Saturday, 10.30am-
5.30pm, Sunday and Bank Holidays 2-
6pm.

Wedgwood Visitor Centre and Museum
Barlaston, Stoke-on-Trent
Tel: Barlaston 3218
Open: April-October, Monday-Friday
9am-5pm, including Bank Holidays;
Saturdays, 10am-4pm.
Facilities include a film show, shop,
museum and refreshment lounge.

A full list of potteries open to the public
is available from the Town Hall, Hanley,
Stoke-on-Trent.
Other factories include Spode China
(Tel: Stoke-on-Trent 46011) and Crown
Staffordshire (Tel: Stoke-on-Trent
45274).
Hanley Museum contains one of the
world's finest collections of ceramics.

Bass Museum of Brewing
Horninglow Street, Burton-on-Trent
Tel: Burton-on-Trent 42031

Chatterley Whitfield Mining Museum
Tunstall, Stoke-on-Trent
Tel: Stoke-on-Trent 813337/8
Open: daily. Last underground trip
leaves 3.30pm approx.
Preserved coalmine with underground
visits.

Styal Country Park
Quarry Bank Mill, Styal, Cheshire
Tel: Wilmslow 527468
A whole village owned by the National
Trust includes a former water driven
cotton mill dating from 1784, now a
museum of the early days of the cotton
industry. Quarry Bank Mill is claimed to
be the best surviving Georgian cotton
mill and Styal village the least altered
industrial revolution factory colony.

Abbeydale Industrial Hamlet
Abbeydale Road South (A621),
Sheffield
Tel: Sheffield 367731
Open: Mondays-Saturdays, 10am-5pm
and Sunday, 11am-5pm. Café open
Easter-September.
Restored waterpowered eighteenth
century scythe and steelworks, with four
waterwheels, tilt hammers, hand forges,
workmen's cottage and manager's
house. There are occasional working
days.

Hardwick Hall (National Trust)
Doe Lea, Near Chesterfield
Tel: Chesterfield 950430
Open: April-October only on weekends,
Wednesdays and Thursday plus Bank
Holiday Mondays, 1-5pm.
Magnificent Elizabethan mansion built
by Bess of Hardwick.

Kedleston Hall
Near Derby
Tel: Derby 842191
Open: Easter Sunday, Monday and
Tuesday, then every Sunday from last in

April - last in September, also Mondays
and Tuesdays at Bank Holiday
weekends. Park, gardens and church
12noon-5.30pm; house and museum
1-5.30pm. Stately home by Robert
Adam with outstanding interior and
furniture. Large park and lake with
Canada Geese colony.

Midland Railway Steam Centre
Butterley, Ripley
Collection of railwayana, locomotives
and rolling stock dedicated to the
Midland Railway. Regular steam trains
operated.

ACCOMMODATION
========

Lists of various types of accommodation
may be obtained from information
offices. Lists are prepared by the Peak
Park Joint Planning Board and the
district councils of Staffordshire
Moorlands, West Derbyshire and High
Peak. The tourist board guides may be
confusing as North West, Yorkshire,
Heart of England and East Midlands
areas all cover different parts of the
Peak.
  There are a number of youth hostels
in the Peak District. You may join the
Youth Hostels Association at the hostel,
and it is advisable to book in advance to
ensure your bed. Family
accommodation is available at some
hostels throughout the year and at the
warden's discretion at other hostels. You
do not need to be a member of the YHA
to stay at Crowden or Hagg Farm.
  Field Study facilities are available at
Eyam, Hartington, Ilam and Gradbach
hostels.
  Further details are available from the
YHA Regional Office, Peak Regional
Group, Bank Road, Matlock, Derbys.
Tel: 0629 4666.
  There are youth hostels at Bakewell,
Bretton, Buxton, Castleton, Crowden,
Dimmingsdale (Oakamoor), Edale,
Elton, Eyam, Gradbach, Hagg Farm

near Ashopton, Hartington,
Hathersage, Ilam, Langsett, Matlock,
Meerbrook, Ravenstor near Millers
Dale, Shining Cliff near Ambergate and
Youlgreave.

TOURIST INFORMATION CENTRES

(*=Information Centres run by the Peak
Park Joint Planning Board)
Ashbourne; 13 Market Place.
  Tel: Ashbourne 43666
*Bakewell; Old Market Hall.
  Tel: Bakewell 3227
Bakewell; National Park Office,
  Baslow Road, Bakewell.
  Tel: Bakewell 4321
Buxton; The Crescent.
  Tel: Buxton 5106
*Castleton; Castle Street.
  Tel: Hope Valley 20679
Congleton; Market Square.
  Tel: Congleton 71095
*Edale; Fieldhead.
  Tel: Hope Valley 70207
Glossop; Railway Station.
  Tel: Glossop 5920
*Goyt Valley; Derbyshire Bridge.
  No telephone.
  Easter-September, Sunday and Bank
  Holiday Mondays.
*Hartington/Railway Station.
  No telephone.
  Open: Easter-September. Saturday,
  Sunday and Bank Holiday Mondays.
Ilam Hall; National Trust Information
  Centre, Ilam, Near Ashbourne.
  Tel: Thorpe Cloud 245
Leek; New Stockwell House,
  Stockwell Street.
  Tel: Leek 385181
Macclesfield; Town Hall, Market Place.
  Tel: Macclesfield 21955
Matlock Bath; The Pavilion.
  Tel: Matlock 55082
Sheffield; Central Library.
  Tel: Sheffield 734760
Chesterfield; Information and
  Heritage Centre, Low Pavement.
  Tel: Chesterfield 207777/8

Regional Tourist Boards
East Midlands Tourist Board,
  Exchequergate, Lincoln, LN2 1PZ
  Tel: 0522 31521
Heart of England Tourist Board,
  PO Box 15, Worcester WR1 2JT
  Tel: 0905 29511
Yorkshire and Humberside Tourist
  Board, 312 Tadcaster Road, York.
  Tel: 0904 707961
North West Tourist Board,
  The Last Drop Village, Bromley
  Cross, Bolton, Lancs.
  Tel: 0204 591511

Peak Park Joint Planning Board
Head Office: Aldern House, Baslow
  Road, Bakewell, Derbys DE4 1AE
  Tel: Bakewell 4321

The Board also run a wide range of
residential courses at Losehill Hall.
For details on courses available write to:
The Principal, Peak National Park
Study Centre, Losehill Hall, Castleton,
Derbys, S30 2WB
Tel: Hope Valley 20373

National Trust
East Midlands Regional Office:
  Clumber Stableyard, Worksop, Notts.
  S80 3BE.
  Tel: Worksop 486411

BIBLIOGRAPHY

Perhaps the most important group of
books published on the Peak District in
recent years are:

The Peak District Millward and
  Robinson, (Eyre Methuen, 1975)
Peakland Roads and Trackways A.E. &
  E.M. Dodd, (Moorland Publishing,
  revised edition 1980)
Freedom to Roam Hill, (Moorland
  Publishing, 1980)
The Peak District Christian, (David and
  Charles, 1976)
The Peak District, Edwards (New

Naturalist Series) (Collins, hardback 1972; Fontana, paperback 1973)
Derbyshire Christian, (Batsford, 1978)
Wild Flowers and other plants of the Peak District Anderson & Shimwell, (Moorland Publishing, 1981)

Other books worth reading are:

Birds of Derbyshire Frost, (Moorland Publishing, 1978)
Peak District National Guide (HMSO, 1960)
The Peak District Banks, (Hale, 1975)
The Buildings of England, Volumes for Derbyshire and Staffordshire. Pevsner, (Penguin, 1978 and 1974)
Bygone Days in the Peak District Porter and Fowkes, (Moorland Publishing, 1979)
Dovedale and the Manifold Valley Spencer and Porter, (Moorland Publishing, 1975)
Churnet Valley and Alton Towers Porter and Landon, (Moorland Publishing, 1977)
Curiosities of the Peak District Rodgers, (Moorland Publishing, 1979)
Ten Years' Digging in Celtic and Saxon Gravehills (1861) Bateman, (Moorland Reprints, 1978)
Peakland Lead Mines and Miners Parker and Willies, (Moorland Publishing, 1979)
First and Last (Peak Park Joint Planning Board, 1978)
The Peak District Calendar of Events Woodall, (published by author, 1976)
Lead Mining in the Peak District (Peak Park Planning Board, 1983)
Railways in the Peak District Nicholson and Barnes, (Dalesman, 1971)
Famous Derbyshire Homes Merrill, (Dalesman, 1973)
Early Settlement in Derbyshire Whitaker, (Dalesman, 1974)
Walking in the Peak District Porter, (Spurbooks, 1981)
Walking in Derbyshire (Derbyshire Countryside)
The Peakland Way Merrill, (Dalesman)

The Peak Forest Tramway Ripley, (Oakwood Press)
Geological Excursions in the Sheffield Region edit Neves and Downie, (Sheffield University, 1967)
The Staffordshire Moorlands: Pictures from the Past Porter, (Moorland Publishing, 1983)
The Peak District: Pictures from the Past, Porter (Moorland Publishing, 1984)

USEFUL ADDRESSES

British Tourist Authority
Information Centre
64 St James Street
London SW1
Tel 01 499 9325

Camping Club of Great Britain & Ireland
11 Lower Grosvenor Place
London SW1W 0EY
Tel: 01 828 1012

Caravan Club
East Grinstead House
East Grinstead
Sussex RH19 1UA
Tel: 0342 26944

Country-Wide Holidays Association
Birch Heys
Cromwell Range
Manchester M14 6HA
Tel: 061 225 1000

Countryside Commission
John Dower House
Cheltenham
Gloucestershire GL50 3RA
Tel: 0242 521381

Cyclists Touring Club
69 Meadrow
Godalming
Surrey GU7 3HX
Tel: 04868 7217

Department of the Environment
(Ancient Monuments Commission)
25 Savile Row
London W1X 2BT
Tel: 01 734 6010

Holiday Fellowship
142 Great North Way
London NW4 1EG
Tel: 01 203 3381

National Trust
36 Queen Anne's Gate
London SW1H 9AS
Tel: 01 222 9251

Ramblers' Association
1-5 Wandsworth Road
London SW8 2LJ
Tel: 01 582 6878

Royal Society for the Protection of Birds
The Lodge
Sandy
Bedfordshire
Tel: 0767 80551

Society for the Promotion of Nature
Conservation
The Green
Nettleham
Lincoln LN2 2NR
(Information and addresses of local
conservation trusts and nature reserves)
Tel: 0522 752632

Wildfowl Trust
Slimbridge
Gloucester GL2 7BT
Tel: 045 389 333

Youth Hostels Association
Trevelyan House
St Albans
Herts AL1 2DY
Tel: 0727 55215

Index

Abbeydale Industrial
  Hamlet, 57, 147
Abney, 118, 120
Abney Grange, 120
Abney Moor, 112, 120-1
Allgreave, 23
Alport, 56, 60
Alport Bridge, 126, 129
Alport Castles, 126
Alport Dale, 126-7
Alport Mines, 66
Alstonfield, 38-9, 41, 50
Alton Castle, 14, 17-8
Alton Towers, 11, 14-15, 19
  46, 132
Alton Village, 15, 18
Aquae Arnemetiae, 74, 114
Arbor Low, 54-6, 136
Archaeological Sites, 136-7
Ardotalia, 74, 113-14
Arkwright, Sir Richard, 20,
  81, 99-100, 103
Arkwright's Mill, 100, 108,
  137
Ashbourne, 36-7, 42-4, 61
Ashbourne Church, 43-4
Ashford-in-the-water, 56,
  74, 82, 115
Ashopton, 97-8, 127
Axe Edge, 11, 31, 39

Back Forest, 13, 24
Back Tor, 123-4
Bagshaw Dale, 57
Bagshaw Hall, 85
Bagshawe Caverne, 116, 122,
  135
Bakewell, 81, 84-5, 115
Bakewell Church, 81, 85
Bakewell Folk Museum, 132
Bakewell Puddings, 84
Bamford Mill, 138
Barmote Court, 65, 70
Baslow, 95, 98, 103, 105
Baslow Edge, 97, 103
Bateman Collection, 36
Bateman, Thomas, 36, 54, 57
Beam Engine; Cornish Type,
  59, 99
Beeley Bridge, 95
Beeston Tor, 35, 38, 40, 50
Belmont, 28
Benty Grange, 57
Beresford Dale, 31, 38-9, 50
Biggin Dale, 37
Bincliffe Wood, 50
Birchinlee, 98
Birchinlee Pasture, 129
Birchover, 67
Black Rocks, 62-4, 99
Black Rocks Trail, 70, 134
Blackley Clough, 89, 114

Bleaklow, 112, 125
Bleaklow Head, 129
Blore, 22
Blue John Cavern, 116, 135
Blue John Mine, 115
Blue John Stone, 75, 115-16,
  118
Bolehill, 64
Booth, Catherine, 44
Boothby, Penelope, 44
Bosley Cloud, 13, 15, 26, 28
Boswell, 43
Bradford Dale, 54, 56-7, 60,
  70
Bradwell, 112, 116, 122
Bradwell Edge, 112
Bradwell Moor, 112, 117
Bretton, 121
Bretton Brook, 120-1
Bretton Clough, 121
Bridestones, 13, 28
Bridestones Chambered
  Tomb, 136
Bridlepaths, 9, 13
Brindley, James, 20, 92, 116
Brindley Mill, Leek, 14-15,
  22, 139
Brontë, Charlotte, 100
Brough, 113
Brund, 53
Brund Mill, 39
Bugsworth Basin, 75, 138
Bunster Hill, 49-50
Burbage Brook, 97
Burial Mounds, 13, 74
Burr Tor, 74
Butterton, 39, 52
Buxton, 74-5
Buxton Micrarium, 75, 132
Buxton Musem, 74-5, 113,
  115, 132

Caldon Canal, 15, 17, 27,
  138-9
Calton, 39
Calton Lees Picnic Area, 106
Calver, 95
Calver Mill, 103, 138
Calver Sough, 104
Canal Cruises, 142
Canalside Pub, 16
Canoeing, 24
Cantrell, Thomas, 39
Carl Wark, Iron Age Fort,
  97, 109, 101, 136
Carr, John, 75
Carsington Reservoir, 44
Carter's Mill, 59
Castern Hall, 50
Castleton, 113, 115-16, 124
Castleton Garland
  Ceremony, 92
Cat and Fiddle Inn, 21, 23-4
Cathedral of the Peak, 76, 92
Caudwell's Mill, 103, 137

Cauldon Lowe, 17
Cave Dale, 115-16, 123
Cave Rescue, 115
Cavendish Mill, 119
Cavendish, William, 104
Chantrey, Francis, 47
Chatsworth, 87, 115
Chatsworth Farm Shop,
  103, 132
Chatsworth House, 98, 103,
  132
Chatsworth Park, 106
Chatterley Whitfield Mining
  Museum, 132
Cheadle Roman Catholic
  Church, 14
Cheddleton, 12, 15-16, 20, 27
Cheddleton Church, 14
Cheddleton Flint Mill, 22
Chee Dale, 73, 76, 79, 83, 93
Chelmorton, 54, 64
Chrome Hill, 33-4, 41
Churnet Valley, 11, 14-19, 27
Clapper Bridge, 60
Cleulow Cross, 26
Clough Brook, 13, 24-5, 29
Coldharbour Moor, 113, 126
Coldwall Bridge, 35
Compleat Angler, 39, 41
Congreave, William, 47
Conksbury, 60, 71
Conksbury Bridge, 72
Consall Forge, 15, 17, 27-8
Coombes Edge, 126
Coombes Valley Nature
  Reserve, 27, 134
Copperworks, 17-18
Cotton, Charles, 31, 39, 41
Cotton Dell, 18
Craft Centres, 145-6
Crag Hall, 25, 28
Crag Inn, 25, 29
Crescent, The, 75-6
Cressbrook Dale, 73, 76, 90
Cressbrook Mill, 76, 79-80,
  138
Crich, 100, 111
Crich Stand, 111
Cromford, 100, 108
Cromford and the High Peak
  Railway, 26, 42, 61-2, 99,
  138
Cromford Bridge, 95, 100
Cromford Canal, 61, 99-100,
  109, 138
Cromford Sough, 109
Cromford Wharf, 62
Crowdecote, 31, 33, 53
Crowden, 125, 130
Croxden Abbey, 136
Crushing circle, 116
Cucklet Delf, 118
Cumberland Clough, 25, 29
Curbar Edge, 97, 103

Cycle Hire, 144
Dane Valley, 11, 13, 20-3, 28
Danebridge, 13, 24-5, 26, 29
Darley Bridge, 95
Deep Dale, 73
Deer Park, 28
Denford, 16-17
Derby Cheese, 141
Derbyshire Bridge, 29
Derwent, 98
Derwent Church, 122
Derwent Hall, 98
Derwent Reservoir, 97, 99, 130
Derwent, River, 54, 95
Derwent Village, 100
Devil's Staircase, 28
Devonshire, Duke of, 38-9, 75, 98-9, 103, 116, 126
Devonshire Royal Hospital, 76
Dieulacresse Abbey, 13, 26, 29
Dimmings Dale, 19, 29
Dinting Railway Centre, 133
Disabled, paths for, 27,52
Disabled, toilets for, 139-40
Discovery Trails, 135
Doctors Gate, 113, 126
Dog and Partridge Inn, 131
Double Sunset, 15, 27
Dovedale, 7, 9, 34, 50-1
Dowel Dale, 36
Dowlow Quarry, 61
Doxey Pool, 11
Ducking Stool, 14

Eagle and Child, 30
Ecton, 38-9, 41, 50, 105, 117
Ecton Mine, 41, 116-17
Edale, 112, 122, 124, 129
Edale Cross, 129
Edale Valley, 112, 122
Edensor, 103
Edge Top, 32
Eldon Hole, 124
Emperor Fountain, 103
Endon Well Dressings, 30
Errwood Hall, 21, 26, 29
Errwood Hall Trail, 134
Errwood Reservoir, 13, 26, 29
Europa Nostra Medal, 70
Eyam, 118-20, 122
Eyam Dale, 118
Eyam Edge, 112, 119-20, 122
Eyam Moor, 103, 119-20
Eyam Museum, 133

Fairholme, 97, 100
Farley, 18
Featherbed Moss, 95
Fernilee Reservoir, 13, 26
Festivals, 144
Fin Cop, 74
Fishing, 140-1
Fishing House, 40, 109

Five Wells, 74
Five Wells Chambered Tombs, 136
Flag Dale, 78
Flash, 22-3, 26, 28
Flash Bar, 28, 41
Flintmills, 15-16
Flouch Inn, 125
Foolow, 92-3, 120, 122
Forest Chapel, 14, 27
Fox Hole Cave, 37
Foxfield Light Railway, 17, 133, 16
Friden, 41, 62, 72
Fritton, Mary, 26
Froggatt Edge, 97, 103
Froghall, 17, 27
Froghall Incline, 17-18
Froghall Wharf, 15

Game Fishing, 140
Gardoms Edge, 97, 103
Gawsworth Church, 14
Gawsworth Hall, 14, 29, 133
George Hotel, 90
George Inn, The, 50
Grants Hole, 124
Gib Hill, 54
Gig Hall Bridge, 26
Gilbert, John, 116
Gingerbread Shop, 42
Gladstone Pottery Museum, 147
Glebe Mine, 118-19
Gliding Club, 94, 141-2
Glossop, 114, 126
Glutton Bridge, 41
Golf, 143
Good Luck Lead Mine, 69-70, 139
Gotham Curve, 63
Goyt Valley, 11, 23, 26
Gradbach, 13, 22-4, 26
Gradbach Mill, 23-4, 29
Grains-in-the-water, 130
Grangemill, 74
Great Hucklow, 120-21
Great Rocks Dale, 73, 78
Great Shadow Wood, 82
Green Man and Black's Royal Hotel, 43
Grindleford, 121
Grindleford Station, 97, 101
Grindon, 52
Grindsbrook, 124, 129
Grinlow, 75
Gritstone Mine, 45
Gulliver's Kingdom, 107, 133
Gun Hill, 22

Haddon Hall, 81, 87-88, 105, 133
Hagg Farm, 129-30
Hall Dale, 50
Hamps Valley, 35, 50

Hang Gliding, 142
Hanging Stone, 24
Hanley Museum, 147
Hardwick, Bess of, 104
Hardwick Hall, 147
Harpur Crewe Estate, 38
Harthill Moor, 54-5
Hartington, 33, 35, 50, 53
Hartington Dale, 39
Hartington Mill, 39
Hartington Signal Box, 61, 138
Hartington Station, 44, 49
Hartington Stilton Cheese Factory, 41
Hassop Hall, 81
Hathersage, 97, 115
Hathersage Church, 97-8, 121
Hawksmoor Nature Reserve, 27, 134
Hayfield, 129
Hazelford, 95
Hazlebadge Hall, 120
Hazlehurst Locks, 15-16, 139
Heights of Abraham, 107, 136
Hermits Cave, 56, 136
High Peak Junction, 62, 64
High Peak Trail, 61-2, 135
High Rake Mine, 90
High Wheeldon, 33, 37
Highlow Brook, 121
Highlow Hall, 120
Hill, Howard, 128
Hill, Sir William, 119, 121
Hollins Cross, 114, 123-4
Hollins Hill, 33
Hollinsclough, 31-3
Holme Bank Chert Mine, 81, 138
Holme Bridge, 87
Hoo Brook, 52
Hope Cross, 114
Hope Marsh, 50
Hope Valley, 112, 118
Hopton, 61, 63
Horton Church, 14
Howden Dam, 129
Howden Reservoir, 97-8, 129
Hucklow Edge, 121
Hulme End, 33, 35, 37, 42, 50
Hulme End Station, 138
Hurdlow, 36, 62
Hurdlow Wharf, 61
Hydro, 107

Ilam, 33, 35, 46, 50
Ilam Church, 37
Ilam Hall, 46
Ilam Nature Trail, 134
Ilam Rock, 34, 50
Iron Age Fort, 56, 67
Iron Tors, 50, 99
Izaak Walton Hotel, 50

152

Jacobs Ladder, 129
Jaggers Clough, 26, 130
Jingler Lead Mine, 111
Jodrell Bank Radio
    Telescope, 13
Johnson, Dr, 38, 43

Kedleston, 90
Kedleston Hall, 115, 147
Kinder Downfall, 126, 129
Kinder Reservoir, 129
Kinder Scout, 8, 112, 124-5
Kirkdale, 82

Lady Cross, 131
Ladybower Reservoir, 97-8,
    122
Ladyclough, 126
Ladyside Wood, 52
Ladywash Mine, 119, 121
Lake Dane, 12
Lamaload Reservoir, 26
Langsett, 130
Lathkill Head Cave, 54, 57
Lathkill Lodge, 59, 72
Lathkill Dale, 56-7, 59,
    69-70, 72
Lathkill Dale Lead Mine, 46,
    56
Lawrence, D.H., 60
Lea Hurst, 109
Lea Rhododendron Gardens,
    100, 111, 133
Lead Mines, 9
Lead Mining Display, 107
Leadmill Bridge, 95
Leawood Pumping Station,
    76, 99-100, 137
Leek, 11-15, 27, 30
Leek Parish Church, 14-15
Liffs Low, 37
Little John, 97, 100
Little Longstone, 83
Litton, 92
Litton Mill, 79, 83, 93
Lode Mill, 39
Lomberdale Hall, 57, 72
Long Dale, 44
Longnor, 33-5, 41
Long Rake, 71-2
Longshaw Estate, 97
Longshaw Sheepdog Trials,
    103
Longstone Edge, 120
Lose Hill, 112, 122-4
Losehill Hall, 124
Lud Church, 13, 24, 29
Lutudarum, 44
Lyme Hall, 29
Lyme Hall and Park, 29, 133

Macclesfield, 14, 29
Macclesfield Forest, 26, 30
Magpie Mine, 56, 69, 137
Magpie Sough, 82
Mam Tor, 112-17

Mam Tor Iron Age Fort, 137
Mandale Lead Mine, 56, 59, 69
    137
Manifold Swallets, River, 40
Manifold Valley, 31-9, 50,
    52, 58, 105
Manifold Valley Light
    Railway, 17, 40, 50
Manners, Sir George, 87
Marble mill, 82
Marple Bridge, 75, 138
Market Hall, Bakewell, 81
Mary, Queen of Scots, 75
Masson Mill, 99-100, 138
Matlock, 98-99, 107
Matlock Bath, 66, 107
Matlock Bath Illuminations,
    108
Matlock Bridge, 95
Meadow Place Grange, 56,
    59, 71
Meerbrook, 11, 28-9
Melandra, 74
Mermaid Inn, 11, 22, 27
Mermaid Pool, 11
Middleton-by-Youlgreave,
    54, 57
Middleton-by-Wirksworth,
    69-70
Middleton Dale, 119
Middleton Top Engine
    House, 62
Middleton Top Winding
    Engine, 63, 70, 137
Midland Railway Steam
    Centre, 133
Millers Dale, 76, 78-9, 93
Mill Dale, 34, 141
Millstone Edge, 97, 99
Minninglow, 62-3
Mock Beggar's Hall, 56
Mompesson, William, 118,
    121
Mompesson's Well, 119, 121
Monks Dale, 73, 93
Monsal Dale, 73, 76
Monsal Dale Viaduct, 138
Monsal Head, 81, 84
Monsal Trail, 76, 83, 134
Monyash, 54, 57, 65, 72
Moot Hall, Wirksworth, 69-70
Morridge, 11, 22, 27, 35
Morris, William, 38
Moscar, 104
Mountain Cottage, 60
Musden Grange, 38

Narrow Boat Trips, 25
Narrowdale, 50
National Park Information
    Office, The, 82
Natural Springs, 84
Nature Reserves and Trails,
    134
Navio, 114

New Engine Mine, 120
Nightingale, Florence, 109
Nine Ladies Stone Circle, 55,
    136
Nine Stones Circle, 56, 136
North Staffordshire Railway
    Museum, 16
North Staffordshire Steam
    Railway Centre, 22, 133

Oakamoor, 27, 29
Odin Mine, 113, 116-17
Offerton Hall, 120-1
Offerton Moor, 121
Okeover Hall, 39
Old Batchelor, 47
Old House Museum, 81, 85
Oliver Hill, 22
Ollerenshaw Collection,
    115-16, 118, 134
One Arch Bridge, 106
Opencast Mining, 69
Opera House, 75
Ossums Cave, 36
Ouzeldon Clough, 129
Over Haddon, 59, 72

Padley Gorge, 97
Padley Wood, 97
Panniers Pool Bridge, 13
Paradise Walk, 47
Parkhouse Hill, 33, 41
Parsley Hay, 42, 54
Parsley Hay Wharf, 44, 61
Pavilion Gardens, 77
Paxton, Joseph, 103, 105
Peacock Hotel, 89
Peak Cavern, 115-16, 136
Peak District Mining
    Museum, 56, 66, 69, 107,
    137
Peak Forest Canal, 75, 142
Peak Park Joint Planning
    Board, 9, 27, 44, 62, 123
Peakland Archaeological
    Society, 37, 137
Peakshole Water, 115, 122
Pennine Way, 8, 124
Peter's Stone, 92
Peveril Castle, 116, 134, 136
Peveril, William, 87, 115
Pevsener, 43, 60, 66, 70, 85
Picnic Places, 139-40
Pike-Watts, David, 47
Pilsbury Castle, 37, 53, 115
Pilsley, 103
Places to Visit, 132-4
Plague Cottage, 118-19
Podmores Flint Mill, 17
Pooles Cavern, 75, 135
Portway, The, 56, 67, 74, 124
Prospect Tower, 107
Pugin A.W.N., 14, 18, 37, 46
Putwell Mine, 83
Pym Chair, 26, 29

Queen Mary's Bower, 105
Ramshaw Rocks, 11, 22
Raper Lodge, 60, 72
Reapsmoor, 41
Redhurst, 35, 52
Redhurst Swallet, 40
Reef Knolls, 41
Regional Tourist Boards, 149
Reservoir Fishing, 140-1
Reverberatory Furnace, 111
Reynard's Arch, 34
Riber Castle, 99
Riber Castle Wildlife Park,
  107, 134
Riding Stables, 143
Roaches, The, 11, 13, 22, 24, 26
Robin Hood, 97, 100
Robin Hood's Cross, 121
Robin Hood's Seat, 121
Robin Hood's Stoop, 121
Robin Hood's Stride, 56, 57,
  67, 74
Rocester, 18
Ropemaker, 115
Rousseau, Jean Jacques, 38
Rowsley, 89-90, 98
Rowsley Bridge, 95
Royal Cave, The, 107, 136
Royal Forest of the Peak,
  115, 120
Rudyard, 12
Rudyard Lake, 12, 26
Rush Laying Ceremony, 14
Rushop Edge, 115, 123-4
Rushton Church, 14
Ruskin, 76
Rutland Arms, 84
Rutland, Duke of, 85, 89, 101
Rutland Mine, 108

Saddleworth Moor, 125
Sailing, 141
St Bertram's Cave, 38
Salters Brook, 131
Saw Mill, 39
Scott, Sir Walter, 88
Sett Valley Trail, 134
Sharpcliffe Hall, 14
Shatton Edge, 121
Shaw, John, 46
Sheen, 33, 52
Sheep Pasture Incline, 64,
  99-100
Sheepwash Bridge, 82
Shining Clough Moss, 129
Shining Tor, 13, 26
Ship Inn, 26
Show Caves, 135-6
Shows, Displays etc., 144
Shrewsbury, Earl of, 46, 75,
  113
Shrovetide Football Match,
  44-5
Shutlingsloe, 25

Silk Museum, 134
Slippery Stones, 97, 100, 131
Smedley, John, 99
Snake Inn, 110, 127
Snake Pass, 125, 127
Snitterton, 67
Solomon's Temple, 75
Sough Top, 56, 74
Speedwell Cavern, 116-17,
  135
Squash Courts, 142
Staffordshire Way, 135
Stanage Edge, 8, 97, 103-4
Stand Wood, 103, 105
Stanshope, 50
Stanton-in-the-Peak, 67
Stanton Moor, 54-5, 67
Stepping Stones, 50, 75
Stoke Ford, 121
Stoke Hall, 104
Stone Edge, 111
Strip field system, 39
Styal Country Park, 132
Sudbury Hall, 134
Swainsley, 39, 52
Swallets, 28
Swimming Pools, 142
Swythamley Estate, 24-5

Taddington Dale, 73, 76, 82
Taddington Village, 74
Talbot, Dr John, 114
Taylor, Dr, 43
Teggs Nose Country Park,
  26, 29
Temple Mine, 107-8, 136
Thornbridge Hall, 81
Thorpe, 22, 61
Thorpe Cloud, 33-4
Thor's Cave, 40, 50, 52
Thor's Cliff, 33
Three Shires Head, 13, 21,
  28-9
Throwley Hall, 39
Tideslow, 74
Tideswell, 76, 90
Tideswell Dale, 73, 76
Tintwistle, 125
Tissington, 38, 44, 47, 61
Tissington Trail, 44, 53, 61,
  134
Tittesworth Reservoir, 11, 28
Toads Mouth Rock, 97, 101
Topley Pike, 73, 76, 78
Tourist Information Centres,
  148-9
Tramway Museum, 100,
  134
Travellers Rest Inn, Flash
  31, 41
Treak Cliff Cavern, 115-17,
  135
Twain, Mark, 38
Two Dales, 85

Underground Canal, 39, 116
Useful Addresses, 150
Uttley, Alison, 111

Vale of Edale, 122
Vernon, Dorothy, 81, 88
Vernon, Sir Richard, 88
Via Gellia, 61, 63
Viaduct, 84
Viator's Bridge, 41
Victoria Cornmill, 86

Wain Stones, 130
Walton, Izaak, 31, 39, 41
Ward, J.B.H., 126
Wardlow Mires, 92
Warslow, 38-9, 52
Warslow Brook, 42, 52
Watchbox, The, 34
Water-Cum-Jolly-Dale, 73,
  76, 79
Water Pressure Engine, 107
Waterhouses, 35, 42, 50
Watts-Russell, Jesse, 46
Wedgwood Visitor Centre
  and Museum, 147
Welldressing, 144
Welldressing, Tissington, 44
Wellington's Monument, 103
Weston Park Museum,
  Sheffield, 57
Wetton, 38, 50, 52
Wettonmill, 35-6, 50, 52
Whatstandwell, 64, 95
Whetstone Edge, 21
White Brow, 129
Whitehough, 14
Wildboarclough, 13, 23, 26,
  29
Willersley Castle, 109
William Clough, 129
Win Hill, 112, 122
Wincle Grange, 14, 26
Windgather Rocks, 13, 26
Winking Eye Rock, 11, 20
Winnats, 115-17
Winster, 54, 57, 64, 66, 84
Winster Market Hall, 54, 66-7
Wirksworth, 64, 69-70
Wirksworth Moor, 63
Wolfscote Dale, 50
Woodhead, 125, 131
Woodhead Reservoir, 130
Woodlands Valley, 97
Wootton Hall, 38
Wormhill, 76, 92
Wye River, 54, 60, 74, 83
Wye Valley, 76-7

Yorkshire Bridge, 95
Youlgreave, 54, 59-60, 65-6
Youlgreave Church, 54
Youlgreave Hall, 65
Youth Hostel Association,
  148, 150

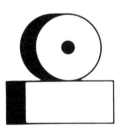

COME GLIDING

AT THE PEAK DISTRICT GLIDING CENTRE.

★Flying membership is open to anyone over 16 years old.

★Training is given in the clubs dual controlled gliders.

★One week residential holiday courses throughout the summer months.

★Visitors welcome — why not come along one week-end.

DERBYSHIRE & LANCASHIRE GLIDING CLUB
MEMBER OF THE BRITISH GLIDING ASSOCIATION.
Camphill, Great Hucklow, Buxton, Derbyshire. SK17 8RQ
Telephone: Buxton (0298) 871270

Callow Hall
Country House
Restaurant

Magnificent rural setting for wedding receptions, functions and conferences.

Delicious food — Extensive Menus — Formal Meals or Buffets.

Fishing Holidays — Self Catering Accommodation.

Please contact Mr & Mrs D. Spencer for a brochure and further details

Ashbourne, Derbyshire
Telephone (0335) 43403

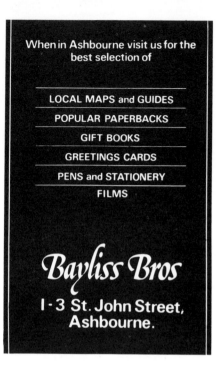

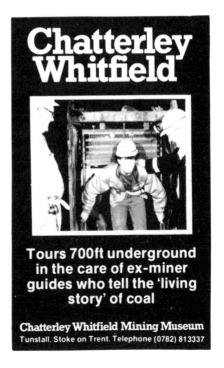